I was standing on the edge of the bank about twenty feet downstream from Wayne when he looked over at me, "Remember that big ole grizzly bear that we have been seeing around here every day for the past several days?"

"Yea, I replied, what about him?"

"Well, he is back again and this time is standing about ten feet behind you!"

"What's he doing?" I asked in a rather high-pitched wavering voice.

"Well, he is just sniffing you out right now. *Oops!* He just took a couple steps closer to you." I peeked over to my right and saw Wayne slowly reach down with his right hand and unsnap the strap on the holster of his .44 magnum pistol.

"Oh great," I thought. "How is he ever going to drop a charging grizzly bear quick-draw cowboy style? I know he is a good shot, but get real; it's my life at stake here."

I whispered over to Wayne "Get ready, he's gonna make a move." I could see Wayne holding his pistol grip, ready to quick draw and fire.

I was trapped and completely at the mercy of this big grizzly's whim. It was going to take a miracle to get me out of this jam. "Dear God," I prayed, "If you are out there, I could sure use a little help right now. This bear is going to attack!"

Big Mac Publishers

Miracles In The Wilderness

Action Packed Adventure, High Speed Crashes, Alaska/Canada Wolf, Grizzly, Moose Attacks.

Or

Surviving Shipwrecks, Glacier Storms, Airplane, Snowmobile, Car, Racing Disasters. Coincidences or Divine Protection?

Tom D. Lynch

Big Mac Publishers
Riverside, California

i

Big Mac Publishers

Copyright

Author: Tom D. Lynch
Editor: Greg Bilbo
Cover Illustration / Design: Adam Lynch
Cover Photos / Mt McKinley, Wolf, Moose, Bear,
Caribou: iStockPhotos.com
Chapter Heading Drawings, Illustrations © 2009   Keith Schneider
Pg 194: AMAZING GRACE (My Chains Are Gone) Words and music by:
John Newton, John P. Rees, Edwin Othello Excell, Chris Tomlin and Louie Giglio

Unless otherwise indicated, Scripture quotations are from:
The Holy Bible, New King James Version © 1984 by Thomas Nelson, Inc.
The Holy Bible, New International Version (NIV) © 1973, 1984 by International Bible Society, used by permission of Zondervan Publishing House
New American Standard Bible (NASB) © 1960, 1977 Lockman Foundation
The Holy Bible, King James Version (KJV)

Library of Congress Control Number: 2009904309
Library of Congress subject headings:
1. Adventures and Adventurers – Alaska
2. Adventures and Adventurers – Canada
3. Outdoor Life – Alaska   4. Outdoor Life – Canada
5. Hunting – Alaska   6. Hunting – Canada

BIASC / BASIC Classification Suggestions:
1. BIO023000   BIOGRAPHY & AUTOBIOGRAPHY / Adventurers & Explorers
2. BIO018000   BIOGRAPHY & AUTOBIOGRAPHY / Religious
3. SPO022000   SPORTS & RECREATION / Hunting
4. REL012040   Religion / Christian Life / Inspirational

ISBN-13: 978-0-9823554-2-8
ISBN-10: 0-9823554-2-4

Published by Big Mac Publishers / www.bigmacpublishers.com / Riverside, California 92504. Printed and bound in the United States of America

Big Mac Publishers

Table of Contents

SPECIAL REVIEW

Tom Lynch has led a fascinating life! I relate because I am a long time Big Game Guide and know the dangers Tom writes about. I assure you, it's a miracle Tom survived. He escaped numerous near-death experiences in his daredevil youth and many more in the perilous wilds of Canada and Alaska. No one is that "lucky." This book is a "thrill a minute" read that will keep your heart pounding right to the end as you discover, along with Tom, a deeper appreciation of life and why Tom is alive and maybe—why you are too.

This book tells a tale of two incredible journeys. The first is Tom Lynch's lifetime of fascinating adventures filled with wild and reckless escapades as a young man, then as an adult in the dangerous wildernesses of Alaska and Canada. The second is a story of a man unwilling to yield to the *possibility* of God until he experienced the *power* of God. Do modern day miracles exist? Draw your own conclusions as you read this terrific book.

Rocky McElveen *"RockStar,"* Alaskan Guide, Nationally Known Speaker, Best Selling Author, *Wild Men, Wild Alaska* and newly released *Wild Men, Wild Alaska II.* (www.alaskan-adventures.com)

Dedication

In Loving Memory:

BERDELL MARIE OPSAL 1922 – 2002

Mom, your unconditional love has meant every-thing to me.
Your Tommy Don

To Mary Jo, the love of my life, and to our four awesome adventurers – Wayne, Bret, Kelly Jo and Adam.

I am truly blessed!
Tom Lynch

Big Mac Publishers

Special Artwork Acknowledgements

Adam Lynch worked diligently on the cover and most of the interior   presentations, teaching himself a new complicated software program in order to create the effects and wonderful cover design.

Keith Schneider worked in a small jail cell, with a 4-inch pencil, no eraser and a cheap pen. Guards would not let us give him better tools. Keith worked in bad light and in an austere environment to create the drawings you see at the beginning of the chapters. We pray he will be blessed both spiritually and physically, as he commits himself to a new life. He is scheduled for release soon.

Foreword

If you've ever had a life interrupting experience and were left without explanation for its outcome, you will connect with Lynch's *Miracles in the Wilderness.* Lynch's book reflects not only on his risky lifestyle and dangerous sense of adventure, it leaves you in great thought about the great and awesome power of our Creator who intervenes in our lives in unimaginable ways. Ways we can only clearly explain when we know Him.

Lynch's story telling style is that of a one who captivates an audience around a campfire leaving them curiously falling into the story with him. Your senses stir, your heart will pound . . . and you will see that aside from the idea of pure luck, there is much more to his story . . . and yours. Throughout his collection of stories, we learn that there is One that watches over us. One who intervenes for some when they least expect it and can't explain it, and for others when they directly ask for it through the power of prayer.

As Lynch tells stories covering years of his life experiences as a tough and hardened outdoorsman, you meet a man that had no explanation for what brought him through many dangerous and life threatening situations. Yet, in spite of this, Lynch holds out on God for years before he begins asking the right questions, "Why did you protect me from all this, Lord? What is it you have planned for me?" He becomes a new man strengthened in his trust and obedience in God. His stories are sure to relate to others looking for answers and purpose.

Life is an adventure for all of us and especially for Lynch! For those that live for the thrill of the outdoors, the thrill of the hunt and the need to be an integrated part of the beauty of the wilderness, this book is for you. By the end of the book, I pray that if you don't already know the Creator, that you would at least look deeply and know that you do have an awesome Creator and He walks along side of you knowing your thoughts, prayers and His plan for your future—always.

Craig Heilman
Executive Pastor / Missions
Door Creek Church, Madison, WI

Introduction

D o you believe in miracles? You know the biblical kind that we all heard so much about as kids. Do you honestly think all those things really happened? Things like the parting of the Red Sea, Jesus walking on water, raising people from the dead and other wild things like that?

In *Miracles,* CS Lewis defines a miracle as "an interference with Nature by supernatural power." Thorndike-Barnhart *Advanced Dictionary* expands its definition of the word miracle to "something marvelous; a wonder."

The Old Testament was written over four-thousand years ago and the New Testament over two-thousand years ago, so even if all those miracles really did occur back then—could they still happen today?

Are there things in today's world that are *interferences with Nature by supernatural powers, or things that are extraordinarily marvelous and wondrous?* If so, they would qualify as modern miracles.

I have been involved in dozens of dangerous crashes and horrific wilderness situations that have tested nature's way to the limits and beyond, yet I am still alive. Were my many escapes from certain death miracles, coincidences or good luck? I would like you to judge.

I have spent years asking, "Why was I saved from certain death so often and for what purpose(s) am I alive today?"

The first two chapters form a background and deal with my pre-wilderness years before I began my odyssey in the wilds. I am not terribly proud of those years, but in my struggle to know the truth, had to be honest with myself.

Please enjoy my crazy journey and resultant conclusions. Quite possibly, there are parallels in your path that will resonate with mine. Read on and find out!

"Our God is a God who saves; from the Sovereign Lord comes escape from death." (PSALM 68:20)

Big Mac Publishers

Daredevil Me

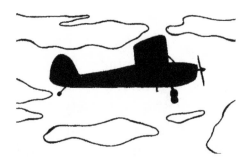

Once, when I was five-years old, our family moved to a farm near Necedah, Wisconsin. There was an old abandoned windmill out near the barn and my two older brothers and I dared each other to see how far up the old rusty metal stairs we had the courage to climb.

We took turns, advancing a little higher than the brother before. Well, after a few turns, I wanted to make sure that I was the winner, so I scampered all the way up to the top, climbed out onto the old rickety wooden planks of the platform, and declared myself king of the world.

I had won, and had beaten both my older brothers in the process, but now I had a problem. I had broken out most of the platform boards near the stairs in my rush to the top and realized that I would have to jump across the opening and grab the stairs on the fly in order to get back down. Pretty scary situation!

My brothers went to get Mom and she was furious with me. "You can just sit there 'till your dad gets home," was her only comment. To tell you the truth, I think she was too afraid of the heights to come up and rescue me. I was pretty high up. I waited for several hours for my dad to get home. He just laughed and shook his head as he climbed up and lifted me across the opening in the platform to safety.

When I was a little older, in Junior High School in fact, I once got another harebrained idea. Every winter the city workers in Sun Prairie, Wisconsin would flood the football field with water so that it would freeze into an ice skating rink. On one side of the field was a long, steep hill that was great for sledding.

I got this idea that if the city workers would spray some water on the hill and let it freeze, we could skate down it to the rink below. Then, if I was to build a ramp out of snow at the bottom, and they were to spray that with water too, we'd have a really neat jump to go over as well. My friends and I made the ramp and managed to talk the city workers into spraying water on our newfound downhill skating track-jump-rink thing for us.

The next morning dawned cold, clear and crisp so off we went for the challenge of the decade, but my, what a challenge it turned out to be. Yikes, that ice hill was fast. We'd probably hit thirty mph by the time we made it to the bottom of the hill and then there was the jump to deal with. We all tried over and over again, but none of us could make it over that ramp without crashing into a heap at landing. Everyone gave up except me. I just had to conquer this hill. It was my idea to build it, so it was up to me to skate it. There could be no turning back.

After about a zillion tries, I finally got myself into a low crouch as I sailed down the incline and then stood upright once I was airborne after clearing the ramp. This allowed me to extend my arms out for balance while in the air, something like a ski jumper would do, which in turn gave my knees ample room to bend upon the impact of landing.

It worked. After landing, I nonchalantly circled the rink in my victory lap before coming to a perfect hockey stop much to the delight of the cheering crowd of people gathered there to watch the spectacle. I then glanced at my watch and told everybody, "gotta go" as I headed off toward home. Truth be told, I was so battered and banged up that I could hardly walk. I was stiff and sore for days. However, I had conquered the hill and I was a hero once again! Crazy, huh?

My wild and crazy spirit didn't mellow out while I was in college, either. During my sophomore year at the University of Wisconsin - Steven's Point I decided that Halloween night needed a little perking up. There was an old World War I cannon parked on display in front of the National Guard Armory on the far side of town that just called out to be moved.

In 1964, cell phones hadn't been invented yet, so I rounded up a team of fraternity brothers with flashlights and posted them at key intersections along the chosen route across town.

Then, at about 3:00 a.m. I hooked the old cannon up to a 1955 Ford convertible and headed toward campus. Boy, those steel wheels made a lot of noise rolling across the pavement. I drove with the lights off. The flashlight signals codes we had worked out at the key intersections were one flash if it was all clear and two if other vehicles were in sight.

At one of the "two-flash" intersections I did notice a squad car drive past up ahead, but we made it all the way to the Campus Union without being stopped. There I deposited our prize on the front steps and everyone had to walk around it to get in the front doors. Was that cool or what? It stayed there for two weeks before the National Guard boys came to fetch it back. They were only a little upset, I think. At least I saw a couple of them laughing.

Later on in life, flying airplanes and driving fast boats provided many of my opportunities for thrills and adventures. I had one flying adventure, however, that became more than just a thrill; it was a near death experience with a miraculous ending.

That particular October in 1979, I had flown my brother, Jim and my dad out to Gillette, Wyoming for a mule deer and antelope hunt. I owned a six-passenger Cherokee Six Piper airplane at the time, which was an awesome machine—fast and powerful.

I had already taken three of the six seats out before we left, in anticipation of returning with a full load of wild game meat and antlers. As it turned out, we needed every bit of space available for the three antelope and three large mule deer that we shot, plus all our gear.

The runway at the Gillette airport was over a mile long, but also about a mile high! At 4,650 feet elevation, the air is thinner and you need more distance to reach lift-off speed than airports that are at or near sea level.

That Sunday morning dawned clear and cool, about forty degrees Fahrenheit, which made it a perfect day to fly home after a successful hunt filled with good times and great hunting. By 7:00 a.m. I had calculated our weight (heavy), density altitude and lift-off speeds prior to take off and had determined that we would need just about all of the runway length to reach a speed that would sustain flight. It was going to be close, but I was flying a strong and powerful airplane that I had a lot of confidence could do the job.

I visually picked out a reference point of no return, meaning that if I hadn't reached lift-off speed of approximately fifty-five mph by the time I reached that spot, I would have just enough time to jam on the brakes and stop before running out of runway.

The only real concern I had was that of manually leaning the fuel-to-air mixture for the carburetor to obtain the best performance level for our altitude. All naturally aspirated airplane engines have fuel mixture controls for high altitude flying but this was my first experience at a mountain take-off.

With all passengers and gear strapped in and ready to go, I fired up the engine and began rotation. As we accelerated down the runway, the airplane was running smooth and gaining speed at a constant rate.

As I approached the visual point of no return, I was accelerating through forty-seven mph, which wasn't the fifty-five that I wanted, but it was pretty close. Besides, the fifty-five-mph number was only a close estimate, but at forty-seven, the *speed gain* slowed. The engine sound flattened out and the RPM's stopped increasing. I immediately suspected that the fuel to air mixture was too rich so I quickly leaned it back a bit, but to no avail.

I quickly scanned all the instruments looking for something out of the ordinary, but found nothing wrong, yet air speed had only increased to forty-eight mph. I needed seven more mph, according to my calculations, to fly that bird, but they just were not there.

All this had transpired in a matter of only a few seconds and we were now past our point of no return and nearly out of runway. I kept the nose down and the throttle pinned to the firewall to gain every possible fraction of a mph before I jerked the controls back, hoping beyond hope that we would lift off. The Cherokee moaned and groaned as it skipped off the last few feet of pavement, but we did go airborne, albeit not by much.

We were flying, but the attitude (orientation to horizon) of the airplane was so close to being vertical that I was afraid we were going to stall and crash at any second. I kept the throttle to the firewall and continued to fiddle with the fuel mixture controls, convinced that we were running too rich for the altitude. I couldn't think of anything else to do because all the gauges indicated that the engine was operating fine.

Somehow the airplane managed to stay in the air, but not very high. We were only ten to fifteen feet above the ground and not gaining. My brother and Dad said nothing. They knew something was seriously wrong and could see the tension in my face as I struggled to keep us airborne and alive. With a full load of eighty-six gallons of one-hundred-octane fuel on board, any crash would be sure to be a fiery one.

Fortunately, Gillette, Wyoming is situated atop a huge plateau and the terrain is about as flat as a pancake. There was nothing but sagebrush and tumbleweeds for miles on end. After about twenty miles of slow, agonizing, near-stall speed flight, my heart leapt to my throat as the four-lane, super-slab of Interstate Highway 90 loomed into sight.

Turning away from the highway was totally out of the question, however, because we were already flying at probably one mph over stall speed and any turn would slow our pace and put us into a tailspin in a nanosecond.

"Oh crap," I said aloud, as numerous overhead power lines came into sight, stretching endlessly from power pole to power pole. *Now what*, I thought. *I can't get over them and I can't turn away from them. No choice but to go under them. This was not good!* At this point, I was covered with perspiration and in a battle for our lives. I yelled, "We are going under them," but there came no reply. Both passengers knew the seriousness of the situation we were in and did not want to affect my concentration.

As we flew closer and closer to the highway and the high line wires, I tried to gauge the breaks in truck traffic because I didn't think there would be room to fit an eighteen-wheeler and the airplane between the pavement and the overhead power lines at the same time.

Good lord, how could there possibly be so many trucks on the road so early on a Sunday morning, I thought. I don't remember any feelings of fear or imminent doom as we approached the transmission lines that Sunday morning. My life didn't flash before my eyes or anything like that. The thought of not making it through alive, never entered my mind. I was just totally focused on gauging the traffic to be able to slip through unscathed.

It was going to be close, real close. Then suddenly without warning and with only a few seconds to spare, the engine screamed to life with increased RPM and we surged upwards into the air. The sudden full power from the three-hundred-horsepower, Lycoming engine literally shot us upward at close to one-thousand feet per minute, up and over the power lines with a good ten feet to spare.

What had just happened? I hadn't a clue. I flew up to about twelve-thousand feet and circled around for a while as I checked all the gauges once again trying to find what had gone wrong. Nothing showed up, so I came to the conclusion that maybe a piece of dirt or something had jammed a valve open causing a lack of compression in one cylinder until it freed itself at the last second.

It never crossed my mind that it might have been celestial intervention that saved our hides. I wasn't much of a believer at that time.

The rest of our return flight to Wisconsin was uneventful. When we got back, I asked a mechanic about the problem we had experienced and he agreed with my guess that it was probably just a stuck valve.

A couple months later, the same problem occurred as I was departing from the Hayward, Wisconsin airport. It was just my wife and me aboard with only a small amount of luggage, so the airplane was light enough to sustain flight until the engine smoothed out again.

Not very scary that time, but still troubling to say the least. When it happened the next day, for the third time in all, flying out of Thunder Bay, Ontario, Canada, I got serious and found a local mechanic that figured out what the problem was. Weak valve springs or possibly lead build-up in the valve guides was his diagnosis.

When the engine was cold and the oil was thick, the valve springs would not close all the way which allowed for blow-by in the cylinders. All I had to do to compensate for that was warm the engine temperature up to at least 170 degrees before take-off, so that the oil was more viscous and the valves would close properly. That was it. I never had a problem like that again for as long as I owned that airplane, but what a thrill ride that was out there in Wyoming—a thrill ride that nearly ended in disaster.

So, do you think God was my co-pilot on that flight or was I just lucky? It could be either, I guess, but I know which way I'm leaning.

General aviation flying is usually pretty safe, but it is not for the faint of heart. You need to be an adventuresome soul to be sure. An old pilot friend of mine once told me that you "must know your own limitations" when it comes to flying airplanes.

Most student pilots never take their first solo flight and a good percentage of those that do manage to do so, scare themselves so badly that they never complete their training and get their pilot license. I know that I have scared myself many times through the years and I had nightmares about those approaching high power lines for a long, long time—but, I still fly airplanes.

My latest plane is a 1948 Cessna 170 that I purchased from a friend of mine in Palmer, Alaska. The 170 is a very popular bush plane. It is a high-winged tail dragger (has two tires up front and a single tire under the rear of the plane), that is excellent for short field take-offs and landings in the bush. Every flight, especially landings, is an adventure with this airplane.

Driving fast boats has been a passion of mine all my life, too. When I was in my early twenties, I once owned a 16-foot-9-inch, Glasspar G-3 ski boat. It was rated for a 50-horsepower motor, but I hung a 90-horsepower Mercury on the transom and dared anybody on Lake Wisconsin to race me.

I actually tilted the engine up to its highest setting for maximum speed and would then "bungee-cord" the hand throttle wide open, so I could *let go* of the steering wheel and crawl up to the front of the boat in order to shift my weight forward enough to get the bow of the boat *down*. Once the bow was down and the boat up on step, I would dash back to the transom, sit next to the engine and literally steer it by hand.

If I sat in the driver's seat and steered the boat normally, I lost a few mph, so I preferred sitting *next* to the engine, this transferred more weight to the aft—thus more speed! It was a little scary and difficult to see where I was going, but man was it fast. What a rush, especially for nighttime racing on the river.

When I turned fifty years old, I finally had enough money to buy a *really* fast boat. A Canadian built 21-foot Cougar tunnel boat with a 300-horsepower, Mercury outboard was truly a 100-mph machine.

What an awesome ride. At about sixty mph, you could actually feel the vessel lift up about two inches as the air would begin to pass all the way through the tunnel of the concaved underbelly of the boat. At this point, the only things touching water were the engine propeller and the trailing ten to twelve inches of the catamaran sides of the boat.

I used a "chopper" prop that by design was trimmed up so that it was only half under water. You can imagine the size of the rooster tail I would throw behind the boat.

Once I had the boat all trimmed up at sixty mph, I would nail the foot pedal throttle to the floor and the boat would literally jump out of the water accelerating to nearly one-hundred mph in just a matter of seconds. The final climb to one hundred was always tricky though. At that speed, I was nearly 100 percent airborne and the slightest headwind could easily send me flipping over backward.

Slowing back down again from such high speeds was a challenge, too. You couldn't just let up on the gas quickly or the boat would go out of control, so you had to ease it back down slowly. I only owned that boat for a couple years however, because my wife, over time, refused to ride with me anymore. I guess it really wasn't too practical considering it had no wind-shield and you needed to wear goggles just to ride in it. Oh well, it was fun while it lasted.

Taking risks for the sake of adventure was inborn for me, but this character flaw isn't necessarily life threatening by itself. Rather it was a very negative atti-tude and an uncaring outlook on life in my early years that took a long time to overcome. Let me explain.

When I was fifteen-years old, my parents got di-vorced and that really rocked my world—hard. I am the youngest of three boys and at that young age, I was in no way able to handle the stress of it all.

Dad had left home and Mom was devastated. She had to scramble to get her life back together and I was too upset and angry to be of any comfort to her. I was confused and hurt. I felt deserted and blamed myself for the family break up. I was the only son left living at home, so I rebelled and left home, too.

I went to Birnamwood, a small town in Northern Wisconsin, to live with my favorite uncle and worked for him in his restaurant. It was a nice get away for a while and my aunt and uncle were very good to me. Not surprisingly, I soon got into a little trouble with the law regarding motor vehicles and got sent back home before I even turned sixteen.

Although I had to live at home, I refused to accept any parental guidance. I rejected all supervision from anyone and lived my life my way, becoming very self-sufficient at an early age.

I was, for all practical purposes, on my own and out of control, by age sixteen. I worked nights bussing dishes at a local supper club, went to school days and pretty much did whatever I wanted in between. My attitude was one of not caring about anything or anyone, including myself. I was in a survival mode, so to speak, with zero self-esteem.

Football was my only real passion. Every year during my four years of high school and two years of college, I would quit smoking and drinking just long enough to get in shape for the football season. That was my sport. I think I still hold the record at Sun Prairie High School where, as a freshman junior varsity quarterback, I threw for seven touchdown passes in the second half of our first game against Columbus H.S.

We were behind six to nothing at halftime, but when I finally convinced our coach, Leon Peddington, to let me start calling my own plays and start throwing the football, that all changed. We won the game forty-two to six and I got moved up to the varsity team the very next day as a tight end, never to play quarterback again. Go figure.

My wild lifestyle was far too consuming during those years. Something had to give. My favorite saying at the time was "Who am I to be denied," which in itself reveals a very selfish outlook on life. I pushed the envelope to the limit—and was doomed for a crash.

The Need For Speed

I was home from college that weekend and it was late at night, about 2:00 a.m. I had been in the bars again and was in a hurry to get to Mom and Stepdad's home when I fell asleep at the wheel.

The last I remember is that I was going between 80 and 100 mph. I went flying off a curve on Highway P, just a few miles south of Mt. Horeb, Wisconsin. The first thing I hit was a telephone pole. The car, a Buick convertible, mowed down two more telephone poles plus all the barbed wire fencing in between before spinning to rest back on the roadway.

I was surprised how far telephone poles are spaced apart in rural Wisconsin. They are between forty and fifty yards—and I hit three of them— and over two-hundred fence-posts right on dead center of that Buick.

The engine was pushed up into my lap and fence posts were jammed up around me everywhere. The convertible top was ripped to shreds from the barbed wire—but I was unscathed. I simply crawled out of the car and walked the one-quarter mile to Mom's house. Not a scratch was on my body.

Oh, I had been in other car wrecks already by age nineteen, but nothing like this. The only question I had the next morning when I saw the wreckage in broad daylight was – why me? Why was I still alive?

There were parts and pieces of that car scattered over a two-hundred yard path of torn up turf. There were downed telephone poles and tangled barbed wire fencing. The front of the car was pushed in about two feet from the impact of the three collisions with the telephone poles, forming a nice "V."

The tops of the telephone poles and electrical wires were all still hanging in the air because the poles had all snapped into three pieces on impact. Why didn't I get hurt? Why did those wires not break? I should have been killed or at least seriously injured, but not a scratch was on my body. Why was I spared?

I took a photograph of that wrecked car and carried it around in my wallet for many years as a reminder of how close to death I had come. I was anything but a Christian at the time, but there was no doubt in my mind that a miracle from God had saved my life that night. There was no other way to explain it.

As I think back on it, acknowledging this fact is what started an intense inner battle for my soul that was to last for many, many years. At age nineteen, I was not a Christian nor did I have any intentions of becoming one.

Oh, I had been through the Lutheran Church catechism classes and all when I was younger, but when our family broke up, I made a conscious decision to go it alone from that point. It was my way of coping and surviving emotionally.

In my mind, I was living only for myself and that was playing right into Satan's hands. He had a pretty good grasp on my soul by then, but now the tables had begun to turn. I began to believe that God had intervened and saved my life! *He* had just thrown a monkey wrench into my grand scheme of life. *He* had interfered with my self-made-man persona in a way that I could not ignore.

I had failed yet God had saved me from certain death with a miracle. I couldn't help but face the fact that I was not 100 percent in control of everything in my life. My hardened outer core of self-reliance had been softened for the first time.

Failure to Yield

Surviving that auto accident in 1964 did have a positive influence. It scared the daylights out of me and slowed me down for a few short years, but unfortunately, I was too wild for caution and sensibility to last very long in my life. It was only eight years later in 1972, that a snowmobile wreck did sideline me, at least for a while.

I was twenty-eight years old, married, had three small children and always in a big hurry. I was self-employed and working day and night. Life for me was make money, buy this, buy that, fly airplanes, race snowmobiles around and drive fast. I was out of control once again.

I owned a 500-horsepower, Yenko Camero, a 100-mph, Yamaha snowmobile and a super-fast, Cherokee airplane. I was terribly independent and answered to no one.

One night while racing around on a Yamaha snowmobile, I had a crash that should have killed me. There wasn't much snow on the ground that night. I hit a small boulder with my left ski at about seventy-five mph that flipped the machine on its side and drove my right shoulder into the frozen turf.

The impact nearly tore my arm right off. Every ligament and tendon was either completely severed or stretched to the limits. My arm simply hung limp at my side. The doctors could not figure out why my neck wasn't broken from such a violent impact. After ten and one-half hours on the operating table and several months of rehab, my neck was still stiff and sore.

God definitely saved my life that night, but I was too stubborn and stupid to realize it. I'll tell you how stupid I was. Only a couple months after the accident, and against doctor's orders, I was hill climbing on a dirt-bike motorcycle near Hayward, Wisconsin.

I took a tumble backward down the hill and the 400-pound, Kawasaki 175 motorcycle landed directly on my sore shoulder. Wow, that hurt, but not nearly as bad as when the doctor took one look at my swollen and hemorrhaged shoulder the next day.

He literally cussed me out and shoved me back down on the hospital bed. "This will teach you to screw up my good work with your stupidity," he proclaimed as he pulled out a scalpel and made three quick slashes across my fresh incision.

I screamed with pain as the blood shot up to the ceiling and I screamed even more when the good doctor crawled up on my chest and pressed down on my wound as hard as he could with a towel to get all the blood out. "There, will that make you listen to me and follow my instructions?" he barked. Believe me, it did!

Right about now you might be thinking that I must be the luckiest and perhaps dumbest person on earth. Two very definite life saving miracles, that to me, were orchestrated by God Almighty, and I was still acting as if I was the only one in control of my life.

I think I really was beginning to get the message about then, but remember; I was a self-made man in my own eyes and had depended only upon myself since age fifteen. God was not prominent in my life back then, but by His grace alone, he was patient with me.

I loved my family dearly, but I was still too much at the center of my own life. So once again, it was my selfishness and overzealous attitude that put me in harm's way. However, I think the Lord pulled me through. He loved me then when I didn't even know Him. What a tremendous love that must be.

I believe He loves us all. I firmly believe that He saves us from catastrophe at times so that we can do good things for him in the future as we are called according to His purpose (Romans 8:28).

You may think these early miracles aren't convincing. Fair enough. We have just begun.

Grizzly Bears

Hunting has always been a big part of my life. Dad got me started when I was very young, only twelve years old, but it was my oldest brother, Gerry that was most instrumental in teaching me the joys and wonders of this sport.

As kids, we lived on a small three-acre plot of land about ten miles west of Sun Prairie, Wisconsin and the open wilderness land adjoining ours was vast (for Wisconsin standards that is), and full of wildlife. During the seasons, we hunted rabbits, squirrel, pheasant, white tailed deer, ducks and geese to our hearts content. Moreover, nothing ever went to waste.

When winter came, my brother ran a "trap line" and would take me with him on occasion. We would get up about 4:30 a.m. drudge through the snow checking dozens of traps for muskrat, beaver and fox on the five-mile-long, trap line, then hustle back in time to make it for the first bell at school. It was a lot of work, but also great fun and a way for our family to survive.

The close bond between my brothers and I had its beginning during those wonderfully innocent early years.

My oldest brother, Gerry moved on to college, but my other brother Jim, our high school buddies and I continued on with our love of the outdoors, seldom missing any opportunity to hunt or fish. Our "big game" species was white-tailed deer, but when Gerry got his masters degree in wild life biology and moved to Edson, Alberta in Canada, the species of big game animals I hunted got much larger, namely moose.

Gerry became a renowned moose specialist through his live trapping exploits and habitat studies in Canada. This wasn't just about hunting. We believed in taking care of, understanding and preserving these majestic monarchs of the north. Gerry's work did much to accomplish that.

Early in his career, Gerry discovered that moose are basically lazy animals while grazing and will walk around a fallen log rather than step over it while feeding. Using this knowledge, he invented a large box trap easily constructed in the bush. He felled trees and cut them into ten-foot lengths for posts and brought in heavy gauge 6-inch x 6-inch wire for the sides of the box fence.

The box measured eight feet in width and about fifteen feet in length, with a hinged trap door attached to the top on each end. More trees were felled to form log fences or wings extending out in a "V" pattern from both ends of the trap. When a browsing moose would happen along one of the log-fenced wings, it would unknowingly be funneled into the trap, and once inside, triggered a spring-loaded trip wire, which would release both end doors to drop, shutting off escape and safely enclosing the moose.

Once a moose was in the trap, the procedure to attach a tag and/or transmitter collar to them was quite delicate. Gerry would sneak up to the trap quietly so as not to spook the animal, then shoot it through the wire cage with a tranquilizer gun. Due to a fear of overdosing the animal and possibly harming it, he would always inject only the minimum amount of drug dosage to immobilize it, leaving the moose quasi-awake.

Once the drug took effect, Gerry would enter the cage and throw a piece of burlap bag over the moose's head to cover its eyes, He would then wrestle it to the ground. It was sort of a cross between a Steve Irwin and a Hulk Hogan move I think, and comical to watch, actually. No matter how large or small the animal was, it never went down easily, even though it was drugged.

Gerry built a dozen of these traps throughout a ten square mile area of central Alberta just northeast of the town of Barrhead. By installing a radio transmitter on each trap with a separate frequency, he could check his receiver from the comfort of his cabin to see if any of the trap doors had been triggered. Gerry live trapped and attached radio transmitter collars and ear tags on literally hundreds of moose throughout his career with the Alberta Fish and Wildlife Department. The wildlife management techniques that he developed from his many years of research are still in use in Alberta today.

Unfortunately, where moose live, so also do grizzly bears. I started hunting Canadian moose with Gerry while in my early twenties and it was virtually impossible for me to go on a hunt with him without encountering bears somewhere along the way.

It was uncanny. I had so many run-ins with these "LTLs" (Long Toothed Lads as the Canadians called them) that my brother used to call me "the bear magnet." Not a very encouraging nickname as I think back on it. We almost always camped in tents and many times would get unwelcomed furry visitors during the night. Some of these visits were pretty scary, but I remember one time in particular that was actually pretty funny, hilarious to Gerry and I, in fact!

Our middle brother, Jim was with Gerry and me that year and we had meat from one moose hanging from trees right next to our tent—in fact only a few feet away. Shortly before 5:00 a.m. that following morning, I awoke to the sound of Gerry stirring next to me as he was crawling out of his sleeping bag and pulling on his boots.

"What's up," I whispered, thinking that he probably just had to go out to urinate or something. "There is a grizzly bear outside getting at our meat," he whispered back. "Get your flashlight ready."

I fumbled around in the dark for a couple seconds before finding it and then Gerry reached down and grabbed hold of his fully loaded 7mm Magnum hunting rifle. Keeping a loaded rifle next to your sleeping bag while tent camping in bear country is normal procedure in the Canadian wilderness. Carrying a pistol in Canada is against the law, otherwise I would most assuredly have had my Smith & Wesson .44 Magnum by my side.

"What's your plan" I asked, as I took a quick look over to my left to see brother Jim still fast asleep and snoring softly. He was all snuggled up in his sleeping bag in the corner of the tent, completely unaware what was going on outside.

"Well" Gerry said softly, in what I felt was sort of a "making a plan as I go" tone of voice. "You unzip the front tent flap zipper slowly, and as quietly as possible. Nudge me when you are ready and then you leap out onto the ground belly down, flip your light on and shine it directly at the hanging meat. The bear is sure to be right there. I'll jump out right behind you and shoot the bear."

I was getting a little tense as I slowly worked the zipper down. *Is this a good plan, or not? That bear is going to be really close. Why don't I get to have the gun?* Then I heard the bear clawing at the meat, so I finished the zipper, gave "Ger" a nudge with my foot and dove out the door just as the loud clang, clang, clang of our alarm clock went off. It was 5:00 a.m.

I flipped the flashlight on just in time to see that ole grizzly bear jump straight up in the air in obvious terror and take off "hell bent for leather" straight over the corner of the tent Jim was sleeping in, trying to head back into the forest.

Trouble was the bear got tangled up in a couple of the tie-down ropes and wound up stomping on Jim who was sound asleep. The bear wasn't about to stop and began partially dragging the tent sideways in his frantic efforts to flee. He finally shook off the tie-downs and beat feet outta there.

What the hey!" Jim yelled as he came awake and scrambled up. He had no clue what was going on and desperately tried to find his way out of the collapsing tent, rolling this way and that, muttering and yelling for help.

Gerry and I had already made it outside and were laughing so hard we couldn't answer him. Finally, Jim found the tent door, poked out his head, eyes bulging wide, hair askew and then seeing us laughing, started laughing too. He vowed to get even.

I don't know who had been more shocked, Jim or the grizzly. I'll never forget the look on that bear's face when that alarm went off. I wonder if he gave up eating moose meat after that. To this day Jim thinks we played a trick on him and still doesn't completely believe our story, but how could anyone possibly make something like that up? Besides Jim had to admit the raw moose meat was chewed up.

On many of our hunts, we would have a number of grizzly bears move in on us so we would have to relocate our camp several miles just to get away from them. One year's events in particular, were unforgettable.

I managed to get myself into a predicament where I was two miles from camp and encountered a sow grizzly with two newborn cubs directly between our campsite and me. They had moved in on a moose kill leaving me trapped late at night in the wilderness.

You see, my brother Jim, "Lucky Ole Jim," as we used to call him and still do today, had gotten a young bull moose on our first day of hunting that year. He didn't call the darn thing in. He didn't track it down. He just sat on a fallen log in the middle of a trail and had the moose simply walk out of the bush right in front of him.

This was not fair at all. I had drawn the longest straw, *the winning straw* and therefore got to hunt with Gerry first. He was the moose expert and knew how to call the big ones in close. I was supposed to get the first shot, but no, Jim nailed one before I so much as saw a *moose fly* in the woods. I could write a complete book about Lucky Ole Jim's uncanny hunting fortune.

Anyway, getting back to the story, after a couple days, both my brothers left me in the bush alone as they went to take the meat to town so that it wouldn't spoil in the warm weather we were experiencing. Late that afternoon, I decided to hunt down the trail a little past where Lucky Ole Jim had scored his kill. *Maybe some of his hunting luck would rub off on me,* I thought.

Just as it was beginning to get dark that evening, I stood up from the stump I was sitting on, which was by the side of the trail. As I did so, I caught the motion of something else standing fully erect at the same time just across the trail from me. It was a beautiful golden blonde-colored grizzly bear no more than fifty feet from me. She had caught my motion just as I had caught hers, and we both stood there looking at each other.

Like most four-legged animals, bears are color-blind and can only see in black, white and gray. I could tell she couldn't pinpoint my presence because of the camouflage clothing I had on blending in with the multi-colored foliage behind me for a background. Bears have terrible eyesight, as you probably know. There was no wind, so she couldn't smell me either.

I just stood there admiring the beauty of the moment. This was during one of my first moose hunting trips and this was my first bear sighting in the wild. She was awesome to behold. Her golden blonde fur glistened brightly in the fading sunlight. Blonde colored grizzlies are quite rare as most are dark brown.

After a few minutes of staring in my direction and sniffing the air, the sow apparently sensed there was no danger and settled back down on all fours again. It was then that the two newborn cubs appeared in the thicket behind her. Now I was really in awe of nature's beauty. It was a real treat watching those two youngsters romp about in play. I guess they were only about thirty to forty pounds each and both were the darker traditional brown in color. I think one cub might have been a boar (male) and the other a sow, since it was significantly smaller.

I noticed one thing about grizzly bears that day, which is different from any other animal I had seen. They have no waist. Seriously. Their bodies seem incapable of bending sideways. When a bear wants to turn to go in a different direction, it will rise up on its hind legs and shift its entire body around to the new direction before dropping back down on all fours again and continuing on. No waist! Guess that might be why the Russian Dancing Bears never performed the Chubby Checker Twist on TV. Remember them? They never twirled hula-hoops either, now that I think about it.

After about ten or fifteen minutes it was really starting to get dark, and I watched the sow rise up to sniff the air once again before leading the two cubs away and along the trail in an easterly direction. With no fear or apprehension, but very naively, I stepped out onto the trail to head back to camp.

I took one quick step forward when it dawned on me that I was going in an easterly direction, too. Oops! In order to reach camp I was going to have to follow and possibly pass that sow grizzly and two cubs, especially if they stopped to feed. This was very unnerving.

As I carefully followed, I realized that the sow had probably scented Jim's moose kill remains, which were just down the trail about a hundred yards or so, and in the direction of camp. She was undoubtedly on her way to it when I initially spotted her. She and her cubs were making a beeline for it now. I would have to sneak past them at some point to get back to camp. Yikes! How could I have been so stupid? Leaving the trail in the dark would be even more treacherous, I reasoned.

The only two things I knew about grizzlies bears at that time were that you *never mess* with a sow with cubs, especially newborn cubs, and you *never mess* with a grizzly's food cache. Now here I was in pitch darkness, without a flashlight, and having to deal with both *never mess,* bear scenarios at the same time.

In spite of their bad eyesight, I knew that bears could see much better than I could in the dark. I couldn't see a blasted thing on such a moonless night. This was not good, either. I wasn't so much in awe of nature's beauty anymore. I was terrified by it. *What was I doing here, anyway?* I thought. *I could be safely hunting squirrels back in Wisconsin, but no, I needed adventure. This adventure just might be my last if I don't figure out how to get out of this jam.*

I tried to remember anything else Gerry had told me about grizzly bears and all I could come up with is "whatever you do never startle a bear in the wild." Okay, so how am I supposed to sneak past that bear, with small cubs and not startle it? Bears have excellent hearing and smell, so what am I to do?

My answer? I decided to make all the noise I could! I started talking loudly, yelling, whistling, stomping and making every noise that I knew how as I hustled along the trail, hoping that I would confuse the bear enough so she would move her cubs out of *danger* and let me pass safely.

Do you realize how difficult it is to talk when you are scared speechless? I began having a loud one-way conversation with the bear, "Hello bear. Nice bear. You have beautiful babies Mrs. Bear. I promise I won't shoot you Mrs. Bear (not that I could have seen her in the dark to shoot her anyway). You aren't hungry, are you nice bear?" If I remember correctly, my voice was much higher pitched than usual that night.

When I reached the kill site and saw the gut pile, I sang, I yelled, I danced and jumped around like a lunatic. Every hair on my body stood at attention expecting that "grizz" to attack at any second. I figured it was now or never.

I kept swirling around in circles with my loaded gun at hip level, fending off attackers like a Japanese warrior. I had the safety off, just in case. I couldn't see two feet in front of me and had enough trouble staying on the trail because I could barely make out the tree lines in the sky on each side. My chances of hitting anything would have been remote.

Once past the kill site, I began to breathe a little easier, but it was still gut wrenching until I made it back to camp and got a fire going. Either I scared the bear away with all the noise I made or the bear simply felt pity on me, the deranged idiot making all those unusual sounds. Maybe, she just didn't want her cubs to eat anything that weird, as it might be deadly. My wife thinks it was my singing that scared the bear away. She claims that I am completely tone deaf.

Whatever the reason, I was back safely in camp and had a raging bonfire going within minutes. I stayed awake all night and kept the fire ablaze. When Gerry returned from town the next morning and saw the huge fire still going he simply asked, "See anything?" We moved camp that day.

On another hunt a few years later when we had a huge boar grizzly prowling about our hunting area, I was left alone in the bush by my brother again. Maybe there was a pattern developing that I never realized at the time. Tom and Gerry on a moose hunt in the Canadian wilderness – grizzly bears move in – brother, Gerry leaves camp.

This time we were about fifty miles north of Barrhead, Alberta and about fifteen miles in from the nearest dirt road. The hunting had been slow for several days due to warm and windy conditions, so Gerry left for a few days. I was on vacation and in no hurry to go anywhere, so I stayed on in case the weather broke and cold temperatures returned.

About 9:00 a.m. I was sneak hunting (stalking slowly and quietly, stopping often to look, hear and search for animals hiding in the brush) along a trail through some really thick alder brush looking for moose sign when I came across fresh grizzly bear tracks in the mud. I could tell by the size of the tracks that it was probably the same big boar that we had been seeing the tracks of, in and around camp for days. They were the biggest bear tracks I had ever seen. The front paw prints were about three times longer than my hand and twice as wide. The claw marks in the mud were probably four inches in front of the pad marks. This was one huge boar grizzly.

The trail I was following through the alders turned into a series of sharp "S" turns winding sharply back and forth. The situation was getting a little tense about then because the alders were impenetrable for sight and the bear tracks were getting more and more frequent. The grizz' seemed to be meandering back and forth along the trail ahead of me. How far ahead of me, I did not know.

The ground was soft and muddy and as I rounded a particular sharp bend in the trail, I noticed that water was oozing *into* the grizzly bear's footprints. Oops! That meant these tracks were fresh, very fresh. This was much closer than I wanted to be to that bear. There was no wind and it was deathly quiet.

I shouldered my rifle and flipped the safety off as I peered into the thick alders in search of anything large and brown. I didn't dare move a muscle because I knew he was close. I noticed the tracks had veered off into the bush to my left. *That's where he must be*, I thought, but still couldn't see him. *Was he circling me?*

After a few moments that seemed like an eternity, a spruce grouse suddenly rose and took flight about twenty feet in front of me. The sudden noise and flapping wings scared the daylights out of me.

If you have ever hunted grouse, you know what I mean. They never take off until you are right on top of them and it's always with a flurry and a lot of racket. Then things got interesting. The grizz', which had only been a few feet away from the grouse all along, took off crashing through the trees in hot pursuit of the grouse. That bear had been about the same distance away as the grouse and I never saw it in the heavy brush. And man! That grizz' could move fast.

Time to exit stage right in haste. I quickly and quietly backed out of that alder thicket as fast as I could. Yowsa, that was close. Thankfully, that big ole grizz' decided to chase the spruce grouse instead of me. Few realize that bears eat all kinds of wildlife. In fact, anything they can catch and they are surprisingly successful at killing a variety of small game. I was definitely inside his "no tolerance zone," in far too close for comfort.

Grizzly bears have no natural enemies in the North Country. Generally, they are curious about humans but rarely attack them, and normally avoid any contact. They usually will not attack unless a person gets too close to them, is a threat to them or their young or invades their food cache. Their 'no tolerance zone" is about thirty to forty feet. Get closer than that and you invite instant attack. If it is a sow with cubs the bear's comfort zone, if you can call it that, is probably larger, (no tolerance area) but each bear is different. There are no set rules in the wilderness!

The only thing I had going for me that day, when I got to within twenty feet of that bear, was the fact that he was already hunting the spruce grouse and had his attention focused elsewhere. Otherwise, I could have become bear scat within a day or two.

I consider this bear encounter and most of the others that I have had through the years as merely adventuresome narrow escapes, incidents that got the heart beating faster. They were scary at times and maybe life threatening to a degree, but nothing that needed or would be viewed as a major miracle to save my life— well, not until the October hunt of 1980 that is.

Miracle in the Wilderness

36
Big Mac Publishers

Alone in the Wilderness

It was just my brother, Gerry and me hunting together that year. We were tent camping in the rolling hill country near Goose Tower, about forty miles North of Barrhead, Alberta, Canada. The weather had turned extremely bad for hunting, meaning that it was very warm and windy, and moose just don't move in such adverse conditions.

Wildlife biologists believe that moose, with those big ten-inch long ears of theirs, can hear at least ten times better than humans can. On a windy day when the leaves are rustling and the tree branches are crashing about, it sounds like a hurricane to a moose. They can't distinguish noises easily with the constant racket in the woods. A pack of wolves or a grizzly can sneak right up on them if they are not careful, so they stand still and continually look around for trouble. It is pretty hard for any predator, including man, to get close to a moose in the wild, when they are that much on alert.

Warm weather is just as bad for moose hunting as windy weather. By mid fall, (September and October), when the rut (males chasing the females), takes place, moose already have their winter fur grown into place. Their hides are about a quarter inch thick and that long black hollow hair they have makes them feel uncomfortably hot when temperatures get above forty degrees. When it is warm and sunny, moose are just too miserable to get romantic. They lay around in the shade all day and will maybe get the "ruttin" feeling during the cool of the evening when it is too dark to hunt them. Maybe I have a country and western song title here, "I've Got That Ruttin Feeling?" Maybe not.

After a couple of days of fruitless sneak hunting, where we would just quietly sneak around the bush trying to spot an unwary moose, Gerry decided that we needed to do some scouting for fresh sign. He told me to walk straight east through the bush for about two miles until I came to a cutline that ran north/south. He would meet me there later in the day.

A cutline is a trail made by oil exploration crews from years past. The oil companies would wait until the dead of winter when the terrain was fully frozen before bringing in their D-9 dozers to clear trails. They drop their blades and mow down everything standing in order to form grid lines every one to two miles apart. After that, they drill seismic testing holes at predetermined intervals for blasting.

By placing seismic testing meters into the ground, it is possible to measure the likelihood of oil being present underground when they set off the charges of dynamite deep into the holes that they had drilled. Alberta Province is literally crisscrossed with these cutlines. Most of them have since been abandoned and reforestation has taken place, but they still provide an excellent means for finding your way around in the Canadian bush country.

Gerry planned to follow cutlines around to the south for three or four miles then circle back east and find me later in the day at the north/south line to which he had sent me. I didn't have a compass, but the sun was out, it was early so all I had to do was walk toward it to the east.

The splendor of God's wilderness in autumn was awesome to behold that morning. The yellow and gold leaves of the birch and aspen trees were dispersed with the bright green of the spruce and pines in a color explosion of breathtaking beauty. The fresh morning dew on the pine boughs seemed to enhance an already effervescent aroma floating thru the forest.

The day, although bright and clear, was a blustery one. There were no sustainable winds to speak of, only strong short bursts coming from several different directions. The bush would turn from dead calm to very loud whenever the swirling wind would pick up and blow the leaves and tree branches about.

Although early in the morning, it was quite warm for late September. I had stripped down to blue jeans, a T-shirt, a light jacket and of course break-up boots, for the short foray into the bush. Break-up boots are lightweight rubber pull-ons that go up to mid-calf and have no buckles. They are ideal for hunting in wet muskeg country.

I was about a mile into the trek when I approached a small clearing in the trees. It was a meadow approximately fifty feet in diameter covered with 4- to 5-foot-tall, marsh grass. Just as I reached the edge of the clearing, and had taken a few steps into it, the blustery wind died down to a dead calm.

Suddenly, a large sow grizzly bear stood up on her hind legs to sniff the air no more than twenty-five feet off to my right, in the center of the clearing. She had scented me, but hadn't seen me. Fortunately, the swirling winds probably made her think I was to the east of her rather than a few feet behind her to the west.

She was a monster, a good nine feet from nose to tail and probably just as long from paw to paw. I was caught in mid-stride and did not dare move or make a sound. I was *definitely* well inside her *no tolerance zone,* and I knew it.

I was in serious danger, which accelerated three-fold when two cubs popped up out of the tall grass near her. The good thing was that they were yearling cubs and the mother would not be quite as protective as she would with newborns. The bad thing was that they were already larger than an average sized adult black bear and I was inside their no tolerance zones too. This could become three against one in a flash.

The situation was very unnerving and my heart started pounding so hard I could hear the beat in my ears.

I eased one hand down and dialed the Weatherby, 3x9 powered riflescope to its lowest setting, silently flipped the safety off and aimed at the back of the big sow. She was so close that the back of her neck filled the entire scope from side to side. I couldn't miss, but if I shot her what would I do about those two cubs, that each weighed at least three-hundred pounds? They could easily be on top of me before I could possibly inject another shell into the chamber. Would they run from the sound of the gunshot, or would they turn and attack once they saw me? That was my dilemma!

I was afraid to move my body. I was caught in mid-stride, facing incorrectly and had to twist to the side in order to hold my gun up to my shoulder and aim it at the bear. As I stood there pondering what to do I could feel myself losing arm strength and balance rapidly.

I was going to have to move my feet soon or fall down, but the air was still dead calm and I didn't dare make a single sound. If one of those cubs spotted me, I would surely be attacked by all three. I would be a goner because they were only fifteen feet away. If the sow turned around, she couldn't help but see me as I was in the wide open, well inside the meadows edge, with nowhere to run or hide.

This was an impossible situation. To be alone in the wilderness and within fifteen to twenty-five feet of three, adult-sized, grizzly bears was definitely incredible. I fervently hoped I would be able to tell someone, anyone about it. It would only make a great story if I could somehow manage to live through it.

For the first time in my life, I felt real fear. My arms were aching from the weight of the rifle and I was beginning to weave back and forth trying to maintain balance.

Dear God, I prayed *I need some help here. I don't want to get killed by these bears and I don't know what to do. Please help me*!

It then came to me that I was going to have to pull the trigger, shoot the sow and take my chances with the cubs. I'd worry later about how to explain to the authorities why I shot a grizzly bear in the back of the neck claiming self-defense. Bear season was not open at the time.

I held my breath and began slowly squeezing the trigger on the weapon as I held the cross hairs on the back of the sow's neck. Just then, as if by magic, the wind picked up. It not only picked up, but it literally howled in the direction of the bears toward me. I loosened the tension on my trigger finger as the sweet sound of rustling leaves, grass and branches filled the air.

I quickly moved my feet to regain balance and squared off to face the charge of the three grizzlies I was sure would happen, but they didn't come. All three of them were now standing on their hind legs sniffing the air and looking away from me to the east, the direction they had likely scented me from earlier.

Now was the chance for escape. I slowly crept backward, carefully placing each foot so as not to make a sound. Slowly, slowly I crept along until I finally reached the edge of the meadow and then I slipped silently into the cover of the forest to the south of them. I had made it. I was alive, but not totally safe yet. Bears can run close to forty-five mph for short distances, so I needed to put some distance between them and me in a hurry. I ran and ran (mostly backward) until I was out of breath and exhausted.

I was wringing wet with sweat as I slumped down on the ground with my back to a big ole cottonwood tree and contemplated what had just transpired. I had actually been within fifteen to twenty-five feet of three dangerous grizzly bears in the wild and had lived to tell about it. Amazing!

Since then, I have thought long and hard about how much at my wits end I had been before I prayed for help. I was truly terrified and my mind was blank as to what I should do. I was helpless until God intervened. He told me what to do and then I firmly believe He brought on the gust of wind, which of course happened to be in the right direction, from them to me. It wasn't just a gust; it was a blast—from nowhere.

I don't think it was just luck that caused that sow grizzly to likely scent me, or whatever caught her attention, from the east when she first stood up, keeping her attention occupied *away* from the west and me. Or just luck that those two near-full-grown cubs didn't see me when I was only a few feet from them. Lastly, it was more than luck that the swirling wind had my scent placed downwind from those bears when it finally picked up again. I believe that it was a miracle from God that saved me that day. I know it in my heart. I was there and lived it.

After resting for a few minutes, I regained my bearings and headed east once again. After a half hour or so, I happened upon a cow moose that was nonchalantly grazing along through the bush. She was alone, so I followed her for an hour or so hoping a bull would come along, but none did. By this time, the sun had disappeared into a newly overcast sky, and I realized that I needed to find that cutline before I got lost.

A compass would have come in handy about then, but I didn't have one so I went on instinct. I eventually found the cutline that my brother told me about and curled up under a spruce tree to take a nap. I was dog-tired. An intense experience can drain you. I was awakened a short time later by my brother kicking at my foot and asking, "See anything?" I just grunted and then told him the story. We moved camp that night.

After I survived something as ominous as I did with those grizzly bears, and having known beyond a shadow of doubt that it was God that saved my life, I was still bothered by the nagging question of why me? I remember praying, *why did you save me God? Why would I deserve this? I am not a particularly righteous man, that's for sure. I don't go to church regularly and I seldom ever pray unless I am scared, so why me? Why was I allowed to live? Why did you create this miracle for me to escape another impossible situation?*

I was twenty-eight years old at the time and had been saved from certain death three times, once from a car wreck, the second from a snowmobile crash and now from three grizzly bears. I had been spared possible death a number of other times, in planes, boats and in the woods. This was causing the inner turmoil for my soul to intensify. I was beginning to sense a greater purpose in life than living only for myself. If I was not important to God, why was he stepping in to save my life in these ways?

Through our many campfire discussions and close personal talks, my brother, Gerry had become well aware of the inner battle being waged inside me. Just being around him had a calming effect on me, I must admit. His personal peace of mind and strong faith was contagious. It hadn't been too many years, maybe eight or ten at the time, since he had found Christ. He could sense the tension in my life, but he also knew that I would have to take that first step to salvation on my own, so he continued to encourage me and pray for me. Wisely, he did not push.

Big Mac Publishers

Lucky Ole Jim

I must digress a bit and tell you more about "Lucky Ole Jim." I have never seen anyone as lucky at hunting as my brother. He started hunting white-tailed deer in Wisconsin at age fourteen using a borrowed twelve-gauge, pump-action shotgun that he got from our uncle Ed. Shooting slugs from a shotgun is hit and miss at best, with longer shots almost out of the question. The barrels are usually not rifled and the slugs are not pointed or accurate, yet Jim got a deer every year for his first ten years running.

To give you a comparison of his hunting luck versus my hunting prowess, let me tell you about one experience I had with a twelve-gauge pump action shotgun.

I was nineteen years old and attending the University of Wisconsin – Stevens Point. I was always broke and in debt trying to pay my own way through school. I was especially broke each year when deer hunting season rolled around. I really missed hunting with my uncles at their cabin near Black River Falls, and this particular year I didn't even own a gun. I had sold everything off so that I could to pay for tuition and books, and that included all my guns.

However, the lure of the hunt was strong, so I scraped up a few dollars and went to a local hardware store that sold hunting supplies. There I purchased an old beat up Mossberg twelve-gauge, pump-action shotgun and five slugs for a whopping total of ten dollars. That was a lot of money for me back in 1964.

It was the eve of opening day, so I only had time to drive over to hunting camp that night. I hoped that the gun was sighted in and functioning properly.

It had been a few years, but I still remembered how to get to my favorite hunting spot for deer and I arrived there long before daylight the next morning. It was a four-foot deep depression in the ground right at the edge of a swamp, something like a boulder hole without the boulder. It was a perfect place to ambush bucks as they came down off the ridges after a night of eating acorns and chasing does.

Right on cue, at about 7:00 a.m. a nice ten-point buck came strolling through the woods within sixty to seventy yards from me. I pulled up on him with that old pump shotgun and pulled the trigger.

Click! It misfired. I quickly ejected that shell and pumped in another round and pulled the trigger. Click! It misfired, too. By then the buck was spooked, but didn't have a clue as to where I was, so he took off running for the presumed safety of the swamp and headed right *toward* me where I was hiding in that boulder hole.

I loaded and pulled the trigger on the rest of the five shells one after the other and they all misfired. Then I grabbed the gun by the barrel and threw it at that buck as he flew past me at a range of about ten feet. Missed him that time, too. Guess ten dollars didn't buy much after all!

Thoroughly disgusted, I stomped out of the woods, got back into the car and drove back to Stevens Point. So much for deer hunting that year. I stewed about my bad luck for months. Nevertheless, Lucky Ole Jim on the other hand, that same opening morning, got a deer, which was I think, his sixth successful year in a row with Uncle Ed's borrowed pump-action shotgun. Ugh! Pure luck.

Once while in High School, Jim went archery hunting for deer near Necedah, Wisconsin. He spotted a small yearly doe out in an open field about 150 yards away, so he stopped the car and told his buddy, Jerry, "Watch this." He got out of the car, strung his bow, aimed about twenty yards high and let an arrow fly. He nailed the deer right through the heart and dropped it dead in its tracks. Unbelievable luck! The normal range for shooting deer with a bow and arrow is between ten and twenty yards and anything over 60 yards is amazing. This was just another instance of Lucky Ole Jim's bizarre hunting luck.

One other time I had both my brothers, Lucky Ole Jim and Gerry, the Canadian moose biologist, up caribou hunting with me in Alaska. Our original plan was to go on a moose hunt up in the Wrangle Mountains where I had been having great success for the past several years. At the last minute, everyone decided that a caribou hunt would be different and more interesting, since we had hunted moose often through the years.

I spent a few weeks researching the Alaska Peninsula herd that wintered in the open tundra near King Salmon, Naknek and Egegik. We were going to be there a little early for the herd's northern migration, which was generally around October 1, but the DNR boys assured me that there would plenty of "bou" in the area for us to hunt.

We flew on Alaska Airlines, from Anchorage to the town of King Salmon, and from there took a floatplane out into the open tundra. Our pilot/guide gave us a quick aerial view of the ten square miles of hunting grounds that would be our home for the next week, before landing on a small lake to drop us off, with our gear and equipment.

The treeless tundra was vast! Miles and miles on end of small lakes, open tundra and an occasional rise of grass covered high ground and bordered on the east by The Arctic Sea's Bristol Bay and the mountainous Katmai Wildlife Refuge to the west. The beauty of it all was breath taking.

His plan was to come back in a week to pick us up, so there we were on our own and without any contact with the civilized world for the next seven days. Awesome!

In Alaska, it is against the law to fly and hunt on the same day, so we spent day 1 just getting our tent camp set up and glassing 'bou in preparation for the next day's hunt. Being that neither Jim nor Gerry had ever hunted Alaskan caribou before, we decided that no one would shoot for at least a day or two so that they could get accustomed to the size of the antlers to help ensure that only trophy animals were taken.

Well, after about only two hours of hunting on day 2, Jim shot one. It was a cow. Female caribou also have antlers, albeit smaller ones normally, and Jim got all excited about seeing something bigger than a white-tailed deer rack, so he shot it. Ugh!

Fortunately, more than one caribou can be harvested with appropriate tags and they don't have to all be bulls, so the cow was legally tagged and processed. It provided some tasty camp meat, at least!

Within the next few days Gerry and I each shot nice bulls that we thought might make the Boone & Crocket record book, but the suddenly "unlucky" Jim had not scored his "second chance" bull as yet.

Later, while out hunting ptarmigan with the shotguns I had brought along, Gerry and I heard Jim shooting about two miles away to the west. Bam, bam, bam the shots rang out. *Oh no*, Gerry and I each thought.

What's he doing shooting at caribou half way to King Salmon when we are pretty much surrounded by them right here where we are. That will be a mammoth pack!

Gerry had shot his 'bou no more than five-hundred yards from camp and I dropped mine within a hundred yards of our tent a couple days earlier. "Oh well," I said. "Let's go get the meat hauling back packs and get out there. I'm sure he will need some help."

Sure enough, Jim had taken a long three-hundred-yard shot at a nice bull and wounded it. Off it had run getting even further away from camp, with Jim running in hot pursuit after his trophy caribou. He eventually caught up to it on the far side of a large lake and finished it off, but we were a good five miles from camp by then.

I looked at the three hundred and fifty pound caribou, thought about the long hike around the lake and then got a brainstorm. I took off the break-up boots, tied a rope around the antlers and headed off wading across the lake, floating the caribou behind. My brothers both thought I was crazy, but I knew these pothole lakes out in tundra country were usually pretty shallow. The water got past waist high a couple of times, but I made it across and saved us about a mile of backpacking labor.

After nearly a full day of lugging the meat and antlers back to camp, I pulled out a tape measure to score Jim's 'bou, and wouldn't you know, it made the Boone

& Crocket record book. Gerry's and mine didn't, but Lucky Ole "second chance" Jim's bull did. Ugh! He got me again.

They say you need a certain amount of luck as well as skill to be a successful hunter, but luck and skill sometimes never come together. This was the case one year when all four of the men in the family, Gerry, Jim, our dad and me went on a mule deer and antelope hunt in Wyoming. We had had a great week with everyone except Jim bagging nice sized mule deer bucks and wall-hanger antelope. Jim, however, couldn't hit the broad side of a barn if he had been inside it that year. All he had to show for the first five days of hunting was a decent sized buck antelope.

So, on the last day of the hunt, while the rest of us were packing up our meat and supplies, our rancher/guide decided to take Jim out for one last try to get him a mule deer.

Wouldn't you know it, they came back an hour later with, by far, the largest buck mule deer taken that year. Uncanny luck! The rancher actually drove right up to within fifty yards of it with his pick-up truck and all Jim had to do was step out and shoot.

The deer didn't even run. It probably thought to itself, *I've seen this dude in action all week and he can't hit squat. I'll just wait until he runs out of ammo and then just mosey on my way.* Well, Jim actually hit the thing and dropped it with one shot. Ugh! He did it again.

Lucky Ole Jim really maxed out his luck on a Canadian moose hunt with Gerry and me one year, though. Without his luck and Gerry's wilderness skills, I don't think he would be alive today. There might also have been a miracle or two thrown in for good measure to get Jim out of the tough spot that he found himself in that fateful night in 1978.

For the third year in a row the three of us plus our dad were going to hunt out of Gerry's cabin in the Alberta wilderness, which was on a small lake about ten miles into the bush from the nearest dirt road. Our point of departure with our off-road machines would once again be a government owned cabin that Gerry at one time worked out of called "the corner cabin."

Before loading up all our gear and equipment onto the two Pass Partout ATV machines, there was about two hours worth of maintenance and repair work that needed to be done on them. Rather than waste all that valuable hunting time, Gerry instructed Jim and Dad to hunt their way in along the cutline that led to the cabin. He and I would service the two machines and pick the guys up later at the first four-way intersection of cutlines, which was about two miles to the north.

When we got to the designated four-way location about 2:00 o'clock that afternoon, only Dad was there waiting. When asked, Dad replied that Jim got bored and decided to take a walk. His plan was to walk the eastern cutline until he came to the first northbound line and then later take the first left and meet up with us back on the main trail.

Gerry didn't like this new development at all, because he knew that the cutlines in this part of Alberta Province didn't run straight or true north/south or east/west. It was very confusing to someone unfamiliar to the area, so we hollered and yelled Jim's name repeatedly, but to no avail. He was already out of sight and sound.

We had no choice but to continue on, and hope that Jim had enough "wilderness" savvy to find his way. We kept hoping that he would show up at any time, but nothing. What did show up however was a bull moose. Sometimes hunting these critters can be so easy!

Gerry and I were each driving our machines down the main trail when all of a sudden a cow moose darted across about thirty feet in front of us. We quickly stopped and I grabbed the rifle, pulled it out of its case and popped in a shell just as the calf scooted across to join its mom. I then raised the gun and aimed it at the precise location that the cow and calf had emerged from and sure enough, a bull suddenly appeared. Before Gerry could say "There's a …" Bam, I nailed him in the neck with one shot and dropped him in his tracks.

Gerry and I gutted, skinned and quartered that moose in record time. In less than an hour, we had it loaded up and were on our way to the cabin once again, but still no sign of our brother Jim. By the time we did get to the cabin it was nearly dark, and much to our chagrin, still no Jim. Where could he possibly be?

We were hoping that he would be there sitting on a stump waiting for us. Then we heard the first signal shot coming from a southeasterly direction. "Boy, he's a long ways away," I said. I grabbed the rifle and signaled back so that Jim knew that we had made contact. We each fired off a couple more signal shots back and forth so that Gerry could try to determine exactly where he was.

Gerry became *very* disturbed! "I think I know where he is and which direction he is headed, and if I'm right, it's not good. Tom, get the boat and motor ready to launch!" The cabin was located on a small lake, about one-mile long and a half-mile wide. I fetched the little ten-horsepower Johnson out of the cabin and quickly strapped it onto the transom of the twelve-foot aluminum boat that was tied up on the bank.

Gerry and I hopped in and he drove us to the edge of the south shore as fast as he could before turning the engine off so we could hear. "Give him one more signal shot, Tom," which I promptly did. Jim answered with what proved to be the last bullet that he had with him.

"Oh no!" Gerry cried out. "I know where he is, and he *is* in big trouble! He is on a northwest bound cutline that dissipates to nothing out into the wilderness. We have to catch up to him, and we must do it fast! Once he loses that cutline to follow he will be hopelessly lost in the miles and miles of endless bush country out there."

Gerry grabbed the tiller and fired up the engine as the race against time began. He motored us about a half mile up the lake to a prominent clearing at a cutline where we stashed the boat and stripped down to blue jeans and T-shirts. We knew we would have to run to catch up with Jim in time and we needed to dress light.

Even though it had turned cold and rain was beginning to fall, Gerry knew we had some miles to run. Although we had flashlights, we still tripped and fell repeatedly over the rough terrain as we sped on at breakneck speed. Our brother's life was at stake! We knew that he had no survival equipment with him since he had left it all with Dad back at that first cutline. With the temperature predicted to dip down below freezing, and this being heavy grizzly bear country, his chances of surviving the night looked pretty slim if we didn't find him.

We ran and ran until we were exhausted, then we ran some more. I was soaking wet from sweat and rain when we finally reached a three-way intersection of cutlines. "Give him a signal shot" Gerry gasped while bending over grasping his knees and panting from exhaustion. I did, but no answer came back. We didn't know that Jim was out of bullets. We repeatedly yelled his name as loud as we could, but no answer.

"He passed by here not long ago; I'm sure of it" Gerry said. How he knew, I'll never know, but he did. "Build a campfire and I'll run him down before he reaches the end of the cutline. He will be hypothermic and will need to be warmed up when I get him back here."

Then, off he ran with renewed energy and speed as I quickly gathered up dry pine boughs from the underside of the many spruce trees, which lined the trail, to build a fire.

"Dear Lord," I prayed. "Please let Gerry find him."

I was beginning to get cold as the temperature continued to drop and I was soaking wet with only a T-shirt on for warmth. I huddled up close to the fire and continued to pray. I wasn't much of a man of faith at that time, but I sure cried out for help just the same.

About an hour had passed since Gerry had left and it was somewhere around midnight, I think, when my two brothers finally appeared out of the darkness and walked into the light of my fire. I jumped for joy and rushed over to hug Jim. He was soaked to the skin and shaking badly from the cold, but he was alive! We spent another half hour just getting him warmed up before dousing the fire and heading back on our long hike to the lake.

Jim's story was one of many errors in judgment coupled with strong survival instincts when it counted most. It was sunny and warm when he first decided to take *a little tour* around the bush, so he left his survival pack and warm coat with Dad. The survival pack was a small knapsack I had put together for him filled with food, matches, water, compass, extra bullets, plastic tarp, flashlight and other essentials for survival in the wilderness.

He *thought* he knew his way around that country, but was dead wrong. When he finally figured out that he was lost his first inclination should have been to backtrack his way out to safety. His real problems however, started when it got dark. For starters, He fell into a blast hole and nearly drowned.

A blast hole is a seemingly bottomless pit usually three to four feet in diameter created by oil exploration crews setting off charges of dynamite for seismic testing. The holes fill up with water and are impossible to see in the dark. So, there Jim was, soaking wet even before the cold rain started. Fortunately, he had enough outdoor smarts to pitch his rifle out to dry ground before he went totally under water as he struggled to keep from drowning.

After surviving the blast hole, his next major problem was the grizzly bear that was stalking him. He could hear the bear in the bush behind him, but could never see it of course, because his flashlight was in his survival pack.

He eventually had a very difficult decision to make. With only one bullet left, should he save it for shooting the grizzly bear if it attacked or respond with one last signal shot? Once again his survival instincts prevailed because we never would have found him if Gerry hadn't heard that last shot when we were at the south shore of the lake.

Jim was terrified that night, but he held it all together and didn't panic. It was pitch dark and he had a hard time staying between the trees and on the trail without a flashlight. He knew that he had to stay on the trail in order for us to find him. He was soaking wet, freezing cold and had a grizzly bear stalking him. Being out of bullets, he knew he was a goner if that bear attacked.

Jim may have made some serious mistakes to get himself into the predicament he was in, but his good survival sense and Gerry's wilderness skills pulled him through.

All this *and* a big helping hand from God, I do believe, is what saved his life. I think Jim would agree today that God provided the miracles that saved his life that night. Even "Lucky Ole Jim" couldn't be that lucky!

Wolf Encounter

I had never been as scared in my life as I was with those three grizzly bears that I had encountered in the meadow on that hunt in 1980. I used to think that it was good for a man to get a little scared once in a while just to know and appreciate that you are still alive. I now know that there are other ways to make that determination.

I would be remiss, however, if I failed to tell you about one other adventure I had that scared the living daylights out of me. I don't know if it was a miracle from God that got me out of this particular predicament, but it may have been. I just don't know enough about wolf behavior to be certain.

Through the years, my brother, Gerry had befriended an old trapper who owned a cabin on an unnamed lake located about eighty miles north and a little east of Whitecourt, in the province of Alberta, Canada. The trapper let Gerry use the cabin for his moose research, so Gerry fixed it up for him. He cut in a couple windows, put a wooden floor in it and rebuilt the roof to keep the rainwater and little critters out.

When the trapper passed away, around 1973, he left the cabin to Gerry in his will.

A few years later, once Gerry's research work had been completed, this area became our main hunting grounds. No more tent camping with the bears from then on. We had solid walls around us at night! The little lake was also full of tasty northern pike, which we caught and thus enjoyed many good meals.

The rolling hill country in this part of Alberta makes for ideal moose habitat. Located approximately 150 miles east of the Canadian Rocky Mountains and about fifty miles south of Lesser Slave Lake, this area, known as Swan Hills, is a remote wilderness, dotted with dozens of small lakes and streams. The flat areas are mostly muskeg, while the hills are covered by aspen and birch trees. Moose love to eat aquatic plants and aspen leaves.

The cabin is located approximately ten miles into the bush from the nearest dirt road, accessible only by eight-wheeled or tracked, bush machines. Four wheelers can't make it through the wet and soft muskeg.

On this particular hunt, Gerry had told me that a couple of moose biologist friends of his had spotted a huge bull moose from the air about three miles north of the cabin, and on the other side of the lake.

We hadn't hunted the other side of the lake before because we never had to. There were plenty of moose on our side, but the thought of bagging a trophy bull of the size they were gushing about, gnawed on me. *Hmm, the challenge would be tough, but why not,* I thought. *I rather like challenges.*

The demographics were not very favorable, however. First, I would have to motor a small boat across the one-half-mile-wide lake to get to a certain trailhead on the other side. Then it would be a one-mile hike on a trail nearly paralleling the north shore before veering off in an easterly direction for another two miles or so before intersecting with a north/south cutline.

The big bull had been seen hanging out near a pothole lake in the middle of some muskeg only a hundred yards from this three-way intersection of trails. I was pumped! This ole "snotbox" was going to be mine (moose have very large snouts and noses, thus the term snotbox).

Hunting this big bull turned out to be a lot of extra work. When hunting out of the cabin, you can sleep in late and only have to step outside and start hunting when the sun was about to rise. The same was true when we hunted out of tents. Now I had to get up about two hours before daybreak to motor across the lake and hike the three miles of trail just to get into position by daybreak and start "calling."

That is how Gerry taught me how to hunt moose, by calling them in during the rutting season. I actually got pretty good at it, if I do say so.

There are two very distinctive calls that you can make. The easiest and most frequently used is the bull call. It is basically a guttural grunting sound made by holding your nose shut with your two index fingers as you make deep guttural grunts into a megaphone made of birch bark. You then thrash your megaphone around on some brush, paw the ground and call some more. What you are doing is actually inviting another bull moose to come in for a fight.

The cow call is made quite differently. It is more like a long, pitiful moan with lots of pitch tone variances. It might sound something like a sheep/cow crossbreed critter that has lost her boyfriend and is sympathetically calling out for companionship.

One call gets bulls coming in wanting to be a lover and the other has them coming in to be a fighter and you hope the moose doesn't get them confused. Cows do not call as much as bulls, so you have to be careful not to be too active and scare a bull away.

Like most antlered animals, moose are nocturnal, so early mornings and late afternoons right up until dark are the best times for hunting them. My first morning out I got the big bull to answer my cow call, but he was not interested in leaving the comfort of his little pothole lake and coming up to the trail I was on.

I later found out why. He already had a cow with him. That meant I'd be making bull calls only from then on to try to make him mad enough to come out and fight for his girlfriend.

The evening hunts were exiting and tricky, to say the least. I would make bull calls right up until it was too dark to shoot and then have the three-mile hike back to the lake, plus the boat ride to deal with. I never carried a flashlight because that would spoil the adventure of trying to stay on the trail in pitch darkness. Only wimps carried flashlights or compasses. I was following my creed that I needed to be scared once in a while just to know I was alive, right? Well, my third night of trying to coax that big bull moose out of thick cover, changed my attitude about what comprises a wimp and what makes good sense for survival.

That morning I had caught a glimpse of him with his cow and he was indeed a huge animal. I could tell his antler spread would easily eclipse sixty-five inches, which is definitely trophy size for a Canadian moose. I didn't get a shot that morning, but I was sure I would that night.

I crawled into the bush on the far side of the three-way trail intersection and finally had him coming right to me by nightfall. He was thrashing branches around with those massive antlers and noisily pawing the ground with his hooves as he bellowed and grunted up a storm. I had really gotten him mad and he was very close, but the brush was so thick, I couldn't see him clearly. I could tell he was only about thirty yards away and just on the other side of the trail. I could even hear him breathing and I could smell him, too.

Big bulls in full rut emit a really rank urine odor. Whew! This guy smelled bad!

It was getting dark fast though, and I couldn't quite make out his shape to take a shot. I needed him to take just one more step out into the open and I'd have him dead to rights. I was tensed up with rifle at the ready and the safety off.

Come on you stubborn old snotbox, one more step and your mine. I gave a coaxing little snort of moose talk to him and eased my trigger finger forward just as I heard the first wolf began to howl. I was shocked! They were only a few yards behind me in the bush. Within a couple seconds, the entire woods erupted with the howling of wolves. I was surrounded by them.

I heard the moose instantly scurry off to the shelter of his pond where he could better defend himself in deep water, but I had nowhere to go. I was trapped. I jumped out onto the trail and spun myself around in circles peering into the darkness but could not see any of the wolves. There seemed to be hundreds of them all howling and running circles around me. (Actually, Gerry knew about this particular pack and guessed the pack was between thirty to forty wolves.)

Right about then I wished that I had been more of a wimp and therefore had a flashlight with me. I would have shot a few of the wolves if I could have seen them. A compass would have been nice, too, in case the wolves blocked the trail back to the lake and I had to venture into the bush. However, one rule of the wilderness is that you *never* leave a trail and venture into the bush at night.

There I was, three miles from safety, on a moonless night with no flashlight, in the middle of a pack of howling wolves. I certainly knew I was alive now, but for how long was becoming questionable. *Oh Lord, why do I have to be such an idiot so often?* I thought. *From now on, I promised myself, (if there is a now on after tonight,) I will never again go into the bush without adequate survival equipment along.*

The wolves didn't seem to be closing in, so I took a deep breath, gulped hard and started off down the trail. As soon as I began moving, the wolves stopped howling. *That's pretty curious*, I thought, but then I figured out why. They were silently circling me. I couldn't see them, but I knew they could see me. Every now and then, I would hear a twig snap or the rustle of some leaves as the wolves continued to keep pace with me as I hustled along the trail.

Yikes, that was unnerving! Why didn't they attack? Wolves are very smart and cunning animals, but apparently, they are not smart enough to know that man cannot see in the dark as they can. Man is their only predator, so maybe they felt cautious about jumping me.

I was mentally exhorting myself, "Predator animals such as wolves like to pursue their quarry, so whatever you do, don't run. Make sure you don't trip over an exposed tree root or a rock or something and fall down, either. Don't give them any sense of vulnerability. Just keep walking fast, stay upright and stay on the trail."

As the minutes passed by, I really began to question my sanity. This was much more adventure than I had ever bargained for. I'm thinking. *Isn't man supposed to be the superior species In Genesis, didn't God put man in charge to rule over all the creatures that move along the ground? If so, then why am I afraid for my life from a pack of His four-legged creatures that are moving along the ground?*

I couldn't remember ever feeling so helpless before. Then I thought of Custer's last stand when he was surrounded by hostile Indians. *He got killed, didn't he?*

Finally, the lakeshore came into sight. I was safe! I leapt into the boat and cast it off in one single motion and was immensely relieved. Wow, that was the longest three miles of my life.

After I motored across the lake and got to the cabin, Gerry was waiting for me at the door with a grin on his face. "See anything?" he asked. He of course had heard the wolves howling and figured that I would have been near them.

So, do you think it was a miracle that those wolves didn't attack? Was it a miracle that I didn't trip over a tree root or a rock, which would have probably provoked an attack? I think we are all likely candidates for miracles, so why not the possibility of one when I was out there surrounded by wolves that night?

Do all miracles have to be big miracles like those that we read about when Jesus raised Lazarus from the dead or when Peter walked on water? Was there any "supernatural powers" on display that enabled me to escape from those wolves? I honestly don't think so. Maybe it was providence that saved me. Whatever the explanation though, I do think that God's care and help were definitely in play that night. Of this, I have no doubt.

Miracle in the Wilderness

Big Mac Publishers

Cavalier Canadians

I blame my brother, Gerry for that wolf scare. I admit that it wasn't his idea to go chase after that particular bull moose, and it wasn't his fault that I got surrounded by a pack of wolves, but it was his fault that I didn't have a two-million candle-power flashlight, five compasses, at least a dozen signal flares and an AK-47 fully automatic, heat seeking submachine gun with me for protection. He should have warned me.

Well, maybe I exaggerated a little, but the truth is that the cavalier demeanor of Gerry and his hunting buddies, while in the Canadian wilderness, did rub off on me, too.

You see, to them it was pretty funny if someone got a little scared once in a while. Using flashlights to find your way in the dark was only for wimps. A compass was a crutch for city slicker use only. This is how I learned to hunt moose in the Canadian wilderness, so it's no wonder that I was ill prepared for handling that wolf encounter.

Gerry and his friends were also great practical jokers. Every year that I hunted with them, there was some sort of stunt that they pulled on some unsuspecting soul in the group. The trick they pulled on my brother, Gerry during the "Goose Tower Hunt" of 1975, however, bordered on cruelty.

There were five of us in camp that year, my brother, three of his biologist buddies and myself. Goose tower is located on some high country not too far from Swan Hills in North Central Alberta. After only two days of hunting, we already had two moose hanging when the grizzly bears moved in on us.

The choice was to have me, the bear magnet, take one of the tents and move two miles west and hunt by myself, because the bears would most assuredly leave the meat and follow me, or to pack up and move the entire camp and maybe leave the grizzly bears behind. After much discussion, the decision was made that we would all leave together in appreciation of the fact that I had contributed to the bagging of one of the moose. Thanks guys.

That afternoon we loaded up the "moose gooser" machine with most of the camp equipment, all of the meat and headed west to rid ourselves of the bothersome bears.

The moose gooser was an old John Deer Cleotrack machine powered by a Chevy engine. It looked like an old hay wagon platform with tracks on either side. The driver sat at the very rear of the machine on a tractor seat and steered by pulling on levers. Not too sophisticated, but it worked.

After motoring several miles down the trail, we picked out a new campsite and unloaded our moose meat and gear. It was getting late in the day, so Gerry decided to return to the old camp by himself to fetch the rest of the gear, while the rest of us set up the new tent camp and got the quarters of moose meat hung up on trees.

It was well after dark when we spotted the headlights of the moose gooser and Gerry returning. That's when Morley and Brent decided to pull their trick on my poor unsuspecting brother.

They quickly slipped on down the trail under the cover of darkness and hid in the tall grass waiting for Gerry to pass by. Once he did, they snuck up behind him, roared like grizzly bears and grabbed him by the shoulders yanking him right off the back of the machine. They roared with laughter as Gerry thought for sure that he was going to be eaten by grizzlies.

That is the kind of environment in which I learned to hunt. You best not be faint of heart to hang around with that crew.

Gerry got back at them later though as he secretly chopped up some moose testicles and added them to the stew we had for dinner that night. It was our last night in camp, and our traditional meal of "mung" was to be served. Mung is a compilation of all the leftover food, which is mixed together in one pot for the last evening camp meal. It wasn't 'till after we had all eaten that Gerry told the truth and got the last laugh for that hunt. A number of us suddenly had queasy stomachs!

Thanks a lot! Even the innocent ones became his victims. In retrospect, I wondered why Gerry was so darn picky as he closely examined each spoonful of mung that he ate that night.

I must admit that this type of mischievous behavior rubbed off on me a little bit through the years, too. One year in particular I was especially cruel to my good friend, Ed Tomah from Sun Prairie, Wisconsin.

Gerry and I had gotten this crazy idea of dragging a flat-bottomed Jon boat for two miles through the bush to the banks of the Athabasca River with an all-terrain vehicle that we borrowed called a Catagator. The plan was to float the Catagator across the river by towing it with the Jon boat and hunt moose on the other side. Gerry had scouted the area from the air and it was loaded with bull moose, so the decision was made to go hunt them.

The river crossing didn't go too well. The current was strong and we almost lost the machine in some rapids, but we finally made it. By then it was getting pretty late in the day, so Gerry suggested that I head off down the trail and do some scouting while he and Ed set up camp.

When I came back well after dark, I complained heavily to Gerry that he should have scouted this area out a little better because all I found was grizzly bear sign. Dozens and dozens of bear tracks and not a single sign of moose anywhere. *We are surrounded by bears,* I complained.

Gerry caught on to the charade and weighed in with a litany of bear attack stories that would scare even the most stouthearted rookie. Ed became petrified with fear. I could hardly keep a straight face it was so funny. He pulled out a half pint flask of whiskey and drained it in only about ten bubbles before passing out in his sleeping bag with his loaded rifle laying across his chest. Having booze in the bush was taboo on our hunts and I had no idea Ed had smuggled in that half pint, so we checked to make sure that he didn't have any more before taking his rifle away and getting some sleep for ourselves.

We hunted for five days. Ed unfortunately never got a shot at a bull, but I managed to call in and shoot a good-sized bull that had close to a fifty-inch rack.

I was hunting alone on an east/west bound trail about five miles from our camp. During the waning hours of daylight, I got an answer to the cow call from about three-hundred yards to the south. I must have sounded like a pretty "hot" cow because this ole boy came in "a runnin" with no hesitation. I masterfully coaxed him in to within fifty yards and nailed him with one shot to the heart. He collapsed into a heap like a sack of potatoes, dead on impact.

Now my initiation into the *moose hunters hall of fame* was about to commence—field dressing and skinning a full-grown bull moose all alone and in the dark. However, first things first, which was to give my brother the signal shots that I had a moose down so that he knew to come and find me with the Catagator machine. One shot, count to ten, then follow that with two quick shots in succession. He knew what trail I was hunting on, so it would only be a matter of time before he showed up.

With small flashlight in mouth, I began the nasty task. A thousand-pound moose is no picnic to move around, but by tying off each leg to nearby trees, I could at least get him stabilized. I then slit him open from one end to the other and skinned him clean before removing the viscera and pulling it off to the side. I didn't want to detach any of the quarters though until Gerry showed up with the cheesecloth meat sacks. It's important to keep the meat as clean as possible.

As I was just finishing up, I saw the lights of the Catagator approaching from down the trail so I had to rush out to stop Gerry before he passed me by. Then, what a hassle it was to find the moose again. It was only fifty yards in to the bush, but everything looks different in the dark.

I learned a good lesson that night and that was "never leave a trail after dark and try to find your way around." Even with flashlights, it took us a good twenty minutes to find the moose. Fortunately, we had enough sense to keep the machine running with the lights on so we didn't get lost.

Overall, it was a great hunt. The only thing missing were the grizzly bears. We never saw one during the entire five-day hunt. That was a first, a rare treat to say the least.

In all I spent twelve years hunting moose with my brother and his friends in Canada. We had countless adventures and countless laughs as well. In time, I realized that their rather cavalier attitudes came from their total confidence in their abilities to survive in the Canadian wilderness. They were great pals of each other and I was accepted as one of the group. Bonding that way is hard to duplicate anywhere else.

That was one reason it hit us so hard when a few years later, one of our group, Des Smith was killed in an airplane crash. It was a reminder that what we did was very dangerous and any of us could die at any time. Des is missed by everyone.

As I look back on it, I really cherish those years spent hunting with my brother. A bond formed between us that will last forever. There is something special for men when sharing wilderness adventures together, I think. The danger, the physical challenges, the reliance on one another and the campfires seem to set hunters apart from the everyday mundane lifestyles of the civilized world.

Shooting an animal is not what culminates a successful hunt, not at all. It is the excitement, the danger, the challenge and the camaraderie that makes a hunt successful.

Hunting and experiencing the Creator's wilderness can touch you in other ways too. Gerry, a consummate outdoorsman all his life, had become a true Christian while still in college and he and his wife Janet were always, and still are today, a positive influence on my life. I love them both dearly.

Without Gerry's encouragement and understanding through the years my journey to the Lord, my battle against Satan would definitely have been much longer and more difficult. The bond that formed between us, especially in the wilds, played a major role in opening my eyes to the truth.

I believe that God is in control of everything, and those who give themselves over to Him are cared for through eternity. My brother and his wife are living examples of this. I am sure that God knows the future and He had plans for me. Gerry knew this then, but I did not. Strong willed and stubborn personalities sometimes need a brick wall to fall square on their heads to learn some things, I guess. For me, my brick wall was a series of life saving miracles orchestrated by God. I am so thankful that He didn't give up on me. I'm sure thankful that Gerry didn't either.

Gerry's Miracles

Up close and personal

D o you know anyone who has ever been charged full bore by an angry grizzly bear and lived to tell about it? *Exactly*, and that is because grizzlies are so dangerous. Experiencing especially close brushes with grizzlies and escaping unharmed are rightly equated with being miraculous, but surviving when a grizzly does charge is a miracle beyond all belief.

On day three of our hunt that particular year, Gerry and I were once again plagued by warm and windy weather, which caused the rut to shut down. Our only chance of success was to sneak hunt through the bush to try to catch an unwary bull moose off guard.

I was hunting the high ground north of Gerry's cabin that afternoon, while he opted to prowl around the muskeg country to the west. Along about noon, I heard Gerry shoot. It was only a single shot, but then a short time later I heard his "signal shots" that relayed the message he had downed a moose, one shot followed by two in rapid succession ten seconds later.

I walked back to the cabin and got the Pass Par II ATV machine gassed up and ready, knowing that we had a moose to skin, quarter and haul back. Sure enough, Gerry had snuck up on a young bull that had been resting under an alder bush about a mile and a half out. One shot at less than fifty yards and at least half of our winter supply of meat was secured.

After removing the viscera, Gerry walked back to the cabin to get the machine and me. After driving out to the kill site, we skinned and quartered the young bull and motored back to camp to hang the quarters from our meat pole.

First, we cut out the backstraps for dinner that night. Backstraps are the tasty tenderloins located along the spine in the chest cavities of most all four-legged animals. Pan-seared backstraps, along with some fried potatoes, onions and Boston baked beans, made a meal fit for a king. This would indeed be a welcome change after living on chili, spam and hot-dogs for the past several days.

As nightfall approached, we began contemplating plans for an evening hunt. The weather was still quite warm, but we were hoping that the cooling from the setting sun might spur some bulls into action. That is when Gerry discovered that his watch was missing.

He had draped the watch on an alder branch at the kill site, and had forgotten to pick it up when we left.

"Oh crap, I'll just go back and get it," he said as he headed off back into the bush. "You'd better take your rifle with you" I called out to him. He used to drive me crazy, always traipsing around the bush without having a gun with him.

By this time in his life, Gerry had spent over fifteen years living and working in the Canadian wilderness and never felt the need for carrying a weapon. Cavalier Canadians! However, we had been seeing many grizzly bear tracks around the area all that week and I got a sudden feeling of urgency that he needed some protection.

I knew that he wouldn't listen to this argument, so I switched tactics and pleaded with him, telling him that he just might spot another bull moose to shoot, and would need to have his rifle. He finally, but reluctantly, agreed to this line of reasoning and returned for his weapon before heading out once again. "Partner" hunting wasn't exactly legal in Alberta, but was still a common practice. Two brothers hunting only a short distance apart would not be a flagrant violation of the one-moose, per-hunter regulation, and our families needed the meat. Our plan was that if either of us heard the other shoot, the hunt would be over. We would not risk exceeding our limits even if another moose was "in the sights."

I decided to hunt the north trail again, but knew I wouldn't get very far because darkness was beginning to close in. Within an hour, it was dusk and as I was beginning the return trip back to the cabin, I heard one lone shot ring out from the direction Gerry went. I waited, but the signal shots didn't follow, so I assumed that he had missed. This seemed unusual to me because Gerry rarely, if ever is off the mark once he takes aim.

Gerry had made it out to the kill site, retrieved his watch and then decided to take the long way back to the cabin. It was getting dark and the shortest way back was from the direction he came, but that would mean getting caught out in the open bush with no clear trail after nightfall. It is *never* a good idea to be in the bush after dark unless you are on a cutline or well-marked trail, which he wasn't, so he decided to hustle out to a larger main trail, which he knew he could reach before dark, and then follow it back to the cabin. He was moving quietly in case he spotted a moose.

Gerry wasn't the only one moving quietly. It is amazing how quiet a huge animal like a grizzly can be in heavy brush. Right at dusk and within a couple hundred yards of the main trail Gerry looked up in astonishment to see a monster boar grizzly bear lumbering right toward him at close range. Gerry could tell that the bear, although heading straight at him, seemed to be unaware of his presence because he was looking to the side. However, that would change in a split second, as the bear was already starting to perk its ears up and turn his head toward Gerry, no doubt becoming aware of something in front of him.

Gerry had no time to think. The bear was already inside the "no tolerance zone," and far too close for Gerry to take evasive action. If he turned and ran, the bear would instinctively chase and maul him to death. In open muskeg country, there are no trees to climb, either.

They say the best defense may sometimes be a good offense. Gerry decided to act before it was too late. Quickly and decisively, hoping to catch the bear off guard, he hollered as loud as he could and then Gerry *charged* the bear!

He was screaming at the top of his voice and running right at the bear, but it was too late. At first, the bear came to a surprised halt and reared up on his hind legs—all nine feet and 1400 pounds of him. Then he looked at Gerry who had also come to a halt, all 6 feet and 180 pounds of him. It was not shaping up to be a fair fight! The bear began growling, shaking his massive head and snapping his teeth, a sure sign of major agitation. Maybe the bear was thinking. *Is this puny warrior going to take me on?*

Gerry froze in terror and in awe. They were both standing there glaring at each other. Gerry was thinking fast. O*ops! This plan isn't working. Now what?* Meanwhile the bear was getting madder and madder.

The bear gave Gerry no extra time to think. The huge grizzly hesitated only a moment, deftly dropped back down on all fours, flashed his enormous teeth, roared ferociously and *charged! Straight at Gerry!*

Those animals can move at terrific speeds in a very short time, possibly as much as 45 mph. To Gerry this bear was coming at him at a 100 plus on the dead run and Gerry knew he was going to be knocked into the next century.

Gerry already had his rifle loaded and at the ready. He whipped it to his shoulder, focused on the bear's head, then *unaccountably* aimed a couple inches high and fired. Gerry's wilderness instincts had prevailed. He *knew*, during the split-second he was aiming, *as if his brain had been flashed with instant knowledge* that he had to *scare* the bear rather than shoot it.

A wounded grizzly is something you never want to deal with up close. A big grizzly is tough and very hard to kill. They get very angry when wounded, and if the shot isn't perfect, it won't debilitate them. They will kill you long before they die.

Gerry hoped that the bear would pause at least briefly once the bear heard the shot and maybe even completely stop his charge. If so, this might provide Gerry just enough time to eject that shell, pump in a new one and shoot the bear in the face at point blank range, if it kept coming. It was Gerry's last hope and prayer. It was a false hope.

When Gerry fired over the bear's head, he was so entranced he never heard the shell explode. He felt the rifle buck and began furiously reloading another bullet, all the while watching the bear to see what the rest of each of their lives was going to look like. If the bear kept coming, they both might die. The bear kept coming!

The bear was so close when Gerry fired that the muzzle blast and fire from the barrel of the gun was clearly visible, and the dim light only enhanced this effect. The powder charge and huge report of the gun at that close range made the bear flinch. Seeing the fire from the muzzle coming at his face along with that thunderous sound caused the bear to jerk his head and veer to the side, yet still nearly crashing into Gerry as he went barreling past.

Gerry whirled to see if the bear would stop, reverse and charge again. Gerry was still feverishly trying to reload his weapon. Sadly, Gerry never did get his weapon reloaded in time. Happily, the bear kept on going, tearing up huge swaths of brush as he crashed through the undergrowth, trying to get away from the puny "fire breathing dragon!"

It was well after dark when my brother made it back to the cabin. He says he can't remember how he got there actually. He was still in shock. I was waiting for him just inside the door when he entered. He was white faced, pale and trembling. It was finally my turn to ask, "See anything?"

We talked about this event late into the night. We both agreed that this was more than just a miraculous escape from danger. It was a modern miracle.

We firmly believed that God intervened. Consider this. What prompted me so strongly earlier, to insist that Gerry needed to have his rifle with him when he left to retrieve his watch? It wasn't the first time Gerry had left without his gun, and I had often kept quiet. However, this time, the prompting was powerful, almost spiritual, even to the point of me pleading and making up reasons for Gerry to take his gun!

Moreover, what prompted Gerry to charge the bear and then *shoot to miss?* Decisions made instantaneously, without time to think and with the intense feeling later that they were directed by an outside force. Decisions that can be explained now and even sound rational, but not easily explained then. Never in my life have I ever read or heard about anyone *shooting to miss* when a grizzly is charging them at point blank range. Maybe if the bear is a ways off, but never up that close.

Everything, after the initial confrontation between Gerry and the grizzly, happened in about a three-second, time span, during which a mere mortal can't function fast enough, on what to do next and especially on making the *right* decisions and then acting them out perfectly!

Gerry thinks that he and I have both acquired some pretty strong survival instincts through our many years of wilderness adventures. That could very well be, and those instincts have served us well over time, but we both realize that even if that is the case, they are definitely God given instincts.

Nevertheless, sometimes, some things are greater than learned instincts. Far greater.

God, our co-pilot

Flying in small airplanes close to the ground is a big part of wildlife biology in Canada, a very danger-ous part. After live trapping moose and equipping them with radio transmitter collars, one has to be able to track them with radio receivers from the air in order to study their movements. It is a part of the science of moose management that Gerry hated. Having lost three different men that he had hired through the years, in-cluding his good friend Des Smith, he simply dreaded flying. It was a recipe for dying.

This particular day in December dawned dismal and overcast with a ceiling in the sky of only about five-hundred feet. He was to fly out of Edson, Alberta for the fifth and final day of this particular reconnais-sance study, and he had a bad feeling in his stomach about the whole thing. He had an excellent pilot, but the weather was ominous to say the least, windy, over-cast and cold. He and his pilot headed out anyway. They only had two more moose to locate to complete the project and they were anxious to finish.

They flew approximately twenty miles before lo-cating the first moose and Gerry felt encouraged, but unfortunately the second one was nowhere to be found. They crisscrossed the bush in a checkerboard pattern for several hours, but to no avail.

By then the overcast ceiling was starting to lower even more and Gerry's pilot was beginning to get concerned. They had nearly eighty miles to go to get back to Edson, and precious time was running out. To make matters worse, the overcast sky suddenly turned to fog and mist and they both knew that they were in trouble. They were in the "soup," with visibility growing worse by the second.

The pilot pushed the throttle to the firewall of his Super Cub and flew as fast as he could, hoping to outrun the descending curtain, but the fog kept settling lower and lower. It wasn't long before they were forced down below the treetops and were flying along the cutlines no more than a few feet off the ground. The Edson airport was only about five miles away when disaster loomed. They had come to a "T" in the cutline and flying up and over the trees was not an option.

Even though the pilot was instrument certified to permit flying through clouds, you still need at least 500 feet visibility in order to land an airplane. This heavy soup had zero visibility and once in it he would never be able to see or find the ground again, without crashing at terrific force, into it or any solid object above the ground. The pilot did the only thing that he could do and that was to cut the engine power, hold back on the yoke and let the plane settle into the trees as slowly as possible. The stall speed of this particular Piper Super Cub is about forty-two mph, so that is the speed the pilot slowed to in order to make the plane stop flying and drop out of the air.

The resulting crash ripped both wings off, and doused each passenger, from head to toe, with 87 per cent octane airplane fuel, but incredibly, no fire ensued. All it would have taken was one small spark anywhere and they both would surely have perished in a blaze of fire. As it was, they survived with minor bumps and bruises and were able to walk out to safety on their own.

At that speed, in an aircraft that was light and afforded little in protection compared to a car or truck, if they had hit anything solid, both would have been killed or badly injured. There are no airbags in these planes. The wings instead, had hit the solid trunks of the trees, tearing violently apart, absorbing the force of the impact and the fuselage had remained nearly unscathed. As thick as the trees were, we are convinced it was the hand of God that directed the plane into the tiny space among the tree branches that saved their lives. What a miracle!

Miracle in the Wilderness

90
Big Mac Publishers

Pictures of our Amazing Adventures

Kelly Jo, our family's "champion" fisher

Prince William Sound in mid-May

1948 Cessna 170: bush plane "extraordinaire"

Mt. McKinley from 100 miles South on the
Parks Highway

The "Foxy Roxy" Leaving Port

King salmon fishing on the Deshka River

Big Mac Publishers

Foothills of the Talkeetna Mountains

Our sheep camp was in this grove of pine trees near
Stone Creek

Amazing Adventure Pictures

Two very happy young hunters

This is the bull moose that attacked me

Big Mac Publishers

Whittier Harbor

A family of orcas cruising The Culrose Passage

Lucky Ole Jim with his trophy from the "second chance" caribou

Gerry the "master caper" hard at work

Young Adam test driving a new Badger Bush Master

Isn't someone going to lend a helping hand here?

The Nabesna River crossing

Anyone for a tasty king salmon steak?

Big Mac Publishers

Baiting long-line hooks at low tide

What a catch!

Don't worry, girl - the bear is dead

Talkeetna bluffs cabin

A great day on the Alaska Peninsula

Moose Attack

Have you ever gotten the tables turned on you? Have you ever been the hunter that became the hunted? One might think this can happen with grizzly bears, but can this happen with an angry bull moose? I didn't think so, that is until a wild and wooly experience taught me otherwise.

The hill country surrounding Gerry's wilderness cabin was once again the site of that year's hunt. Although it was late September, the weather had turned nasty, especially for hunting moose, which means it was warm and windy.

Temperatures during the day would hit sixty degrees and above and it wouldn't freeze at night. The rut, that at one time had been going strong, was now totally shut down. It is not only the length of the day that triggers the rut, but also the temperature. When it is warm, the bulls as well as the cow moose become lethargic. If you throw in some windy conditions, the rut really shuts down because these animals all become wary because they can't hear predators.

The last thing you want is uncomfortably hot, lethargic and wary moose when it is hunting season, but that is exactly what we had going for several days.

At least the fishing was good. We'd take the little twelve-foot aluminum boat out every day and catch northern pike by the dozens, to pass the time away while waiting for the weather to break.

After several days of listlessly waiting for a break in the weather pattern, we decided that we could only stay one more day. Work, family and civilization beckoned.

The next day dawned cool and crisp with no wind, perfect conditions. A high-pressure system had unexpectedly moved in overnight and laid a beautiful layer of frost on the ground. At daybreak, the twenty-six degree air felt nippy on the nose, but it sure was welcome.

As the sun popped over the horizon, the forest bristled in brilliance. Every tree and every bush was covered with the crystalline glass of frozen dew in the form of frost. The ground crunched with every step as I carefully headed down the trail for the first calling spot on my agenda, an open knoll overlooking a large muskeg area.

The tactic for hunting bull moose during the rut is to slowly, and as quietly as possible, move from one calling spot to another, at roughly fifty to one-hundred-yard intervals. At each stop, I would perform a moose call for fifteen to twenty minutes before moving on.

On this beautiful morning, I never got past the first calling spot before I got an answer. I was on a slight rise on the cutline and the bull was out in the flat and brushy muskeg. I was giving the fighting call of a bull moose and he was coming in fast and furious, ready for a rumble. The ruckus he was making by crashing his antlers through the brush, pawing the ground and grunting loudly had my heart pounding intensely.

I could tell he was big by the sound of his huge antlers against the underbrush, and he was coming in at breakneck speed. Wow, what a thrill. This is what makes hunting bull moose so exiting.

I pulled the Weatherby .300 magnum up to my shoulder and flipped off the safety. I wanted to be ready to shoot the very second he appeared, but then the unthinkable happened. The bush got instantly silent. Where was he? He had been coming right at me through the muskeg and I was sure he would be in sight, no more than fifty yards away at any second, but no moose appeared.

I was puzzled. *Did I spook him away with a bad sounding call? I didn't think so. Did he catch my scent somehow? Couldn't have, because there was zero wind. Maybe I called too frequently and scared him off. However, he had been doing most of the calling, not me.*

I lowered the rifle to my waist in frustration and thought in puzzlement, *What the hey!* Just then, I caught a glimpse of him, off to my left, sneaking across the cutline. Maybe he had decided that he should silently circle around me, and come up from behind to size me up, before coming in all the way to do battle. Some of the more battle-hardened bull moose are prone to doing that.

I had barely caught sight of him out of the corner of my eye. I pulled up on him and quickly snapped off a shot just as he was disappearing into the alders along the side of the trail.

"That dirty bugger. What a sneak!" I grunted aloud. I figured that I had hit him because he arched his back a little after I shot, but I was afraid I hit him too high above the shoulder blade. If so, he would survive getting nicked and hightail it to safer places. I have a tendency to shoot high when rushed.

I ejected the shell casing and threw another one into the chamber as I tore off up the trail to where I had last seen him, running as quickly as I could in order to catch a glimpse of him. I fervently hoped to get another shot and finish him off.

That bull had other things in mind. He was *waiting* to take a *shot at me* instead. I had indeed stung him high on the shoulder, but it was not a lethal hit. All it did was make him mad. I really should say *madder*—he was already in the mood for a fight.

There I was, clumping up the trail in noisy break-up boots, and there he was, waiting in ten-foot-high, alder brush, ready to ambush me!

When I was in just the right position to his liking, he let out a roar, the sound of which I had never heard before—at least not from a moose! He jumped out of his hiding place and onto the trail, right in front of me. His nostrils were flared wide and his fifty-inch wide antlers were lowered in attack mode and he was lunging directly at me. Yikes, I nearly had a heart attack right then!

An adult bull moose stands seven to eight-feet tall at the shoulders, so you can imagine the frightening thrill of seeing this guy leap up high and come bounding out of those thick alders, charging at me. My heart leapt to my throat as I skidded to a halt. I instinctively raised the rifle and shot, all in one motion and without thinking. Bam! I nailed him right through his brisket and the bullet went straight into his heart. I dropped him like a bad habit and he fell, just *five feet* in front of me, dead on impact. What a miraculous shot!

You always try to avoid shooting any animal head-on because the target of vital organs is so much smaller than a broadside shot, but I had no choice and no time to think. To send that bullet unerringly into his heart took a lot of divine assistance.

It took a couple seconds for me to settle down and catch my breath, but once I did, I let out a war cry that must have sounded like the wild man from Borneo or something. Yeeeehaaaa!

My exhilaration wasn't just about killing the moose. It was from the incredible relief at facing death or at least horrible injury, being pumped up, and also feeling vulnerable and then escaping. It was the miracle of knowing I was still alive and would go home and see my wife and kids again. It was from knowing that we had meat for the winter.

What a thrill! I had hollered so loudly that my brother, Gerry heard me a mile away. He grinned to himself and thought *I guess Tom got a moose.* He was going to ask me when he saw me, "See anything Tom?"

The Alaska Wilderness

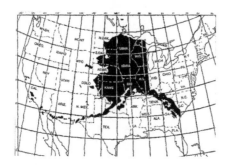

I am convinced that Alaska will always be our countries "last great frontier," unless someone figures out how to build roads over glaciers, that is. At last count there are over two-million lakes in Alaska and the glaciers are too numerous to even attempt counting. With a land mass of nearly 590,000 square miles, Alaska is roughly one-fifth the size of the lower forty-eight states and over twice the size of Texas.

On March 30, 1867, U.S. Secretary of State, William Henry Seward completed the purchase of "Russian America" for the then outlandish price of $7,200,000. The purchase was urged by west coast fishing interests, who had no idea of the gold and oil riches yet to be discovered there.

Seward named the territory Alaska, which is a corruption of Aleut *alaksha* or *alayeksa,* which both mean "a great country." On January 3, 1959, President Eisenhower signed the proclamation granting statehood for our 49th. State.

The Alaska/Canada Highway (Alcan) was built between the months of March and October in 1942 at a cost of $139,000,000. Initially constructed and maintained by the U.S. Military, it was opened to civilian traffic in n1948. It now serves as the major venue for tourism in the state.

In 1980, I packed up my family and moved to Alaska. The "lower forty eight," as Alaskans term it, was in a deep recession and my ceramic tile contracting company was feeling the pain right along with every other construction related business.

Alaska, on the other hand, had recently completed construction of an oil pipeline from the North Slope to Valdez and the revenues were beginning to flow into the economy at a record pace. An economic boom was underway.

The decision to relocate so far away from our home in Wisconsin was a major one. At our family meeting, my wife and all three of my teenagers voted for the move, so it was unanimous. What an adventuresome lot they were! Just mention of the word ALASKA still brings feelings of awe and wonder to all our hearts, even today.

Deciding to move to Alaska was one thing, but actually getting there was another. In 1980, the Alcan Highway was still a re-work in progress. Once you get past Dawson Creek, the terrain is mountainous the rest of the way, and back then the road was nothing more than one curve or switchback after another with *no* guardrails.

On my first trip up the Alcan, I got myself caught in a blizzard near Teslin in the Yukon Territory. It was about 2:00 a.m. in the middle of nowhere and the snow was so deep that I was plowing it with the front bumper of a four-wheel drive Chevy Suburban. There were no tracks in the snow to follow or guide me to keep on the road, as I was the only one crazy enough to be out there that night.

As I was struggling to see where I was going through the maze of switchbacks, I started to notice that on every right turn I could feel and hear a clunking sound coming from the front of the vehicle. After a while, I could swear I felt the left front tire coming loose. *How could that possibly be,* I thought. *I just had a new set of tires installed the day before I left Wisconsin.*

Eventually the problem became so serious that I just had to check it out, so I stopped in the middle of the road and crawled out into the two-foot deep snow and discovered that I had only two lug nuts out of six still on my left front wheel, and they were both almost off. Yikes! This was unnerving to say the least. The mechanic that installed the tires apparently failed to tighten any of the lug nuts on that wheel. If that tire had come off on any right-hand curve, I would most assuredly have plunged to death over the mountain slope. My guardian angel was working overtime.

To solve the problem, I took one lug nut off each of the remaining wheels and put them on the front left, leaving five on each wheel. The next day I made it into Whitehorse where I bought more of them, but what a scare it was that night before.

Later that same winter, about mid April I believe, I was once again traveling up the Alcan to Alaska, but this time driving a thirty-foot motor home. I had it loaded to the max with office equipment, tools and household belongings and was literally flying up the road at seventy mph. It was a bright and clear sunny day, the road was well grooved and in great shape.

During the winter months, the Alcan Highway surface gets a buildup of ice and snow that sometimes reaches a depth of two feet. To help drivers stay on the road, the maintenance crews mount plow blades, with sharp teeth cut into them, on the underbellies of dump trucks and actually groom the roads by making grooves in them.

As I was "Nascar'ing" around a sweeping left hand curve at the base of a large hill, I looked up ahead to see an eighteen-wheeler double-bottom logging truck, which was fully loaded and coming hell bent for leather, right at me. *O Lord, This is not going to work*, I thought. *There is only room for one of us to be side sliding around this curve, and seeing that he was bigger than I was, it would be prudent for me to exit the roadway, post haste.* I pulled the steering wheel hard right, and went flying off into the snow-filled ditch into a cloud of white powder. The truck laid on his air horns contemptuously, as he went flying past me and continued on down the mountain.

So there I was, eighty feet off the road in a field of snow. I opened the door and jumped out only to sink chest deep into the white powder. It took a long time, but I managed to sort of snow swim around to collect all the chains and tow straps I had with me, to see if I had enough to reach the roadway. I was hoping to use them so someone could wench me out. I didn't. I was about twenty feet short.

By then, however, I heard the sound of a truck coming up the road from the south. It was the logger buddy, apparently taking pity on me. He was backing up the mountain to rescue me.

He stopped his truck and came over to me. "Being that I was the one who ran you off into the ditch, the least I could do is come back to pull you out," he said. He had some chains with him and it didn't take long for him to hook on and yank me out of the ditch. In no time, we were both on our merry ways once again, but each definitely traveling at much slower speeds.

Through the years, I have made dozens and dozens of trips up and down the Alcan Highway. I'm happy to say that the rebuilding and straightening of the road is nearly complete. If you have the time, vacationing on the Alcan can be a great experience. In fact, RVs outnumber eighteen-wheelers about ten to one during mid-summer.

I recommend that you make the trip in early June, though. The mosquitoes won't be out yet and the wild animals will be near the roads in great numbers, eating the fresh shoots of spring grasses. Expect to see moose, bison, wild horses, grizzly bears, black bears, deer, caribou, elk and even wolves on your trip.

Plan your trip to be starving hungry when you reach Tok, Alaska so that you have a chance of finishing your meal at Fast Eddies Restaurant. The food is awesome and the quantities are humungous.

One other "must stop" for food is Mukluk Annies near Teslin in the Yukon Territory. The food there is cooked over a wood-fired grill and is nothing short of fantastic. Another attraction you don't want to miss is the hot springs at Laird River.

Living in "the last great frontier" of Alaska was a dream come true for me. Words cannot describe the awesome majesty of that State. The clean fresh air, snow capped mountain peaks, pristine lakes and thousands of square miles of untouched wilderness beckoned my sense of adventure to the max. Most outdoorsmen only dream of living there, but I lived out my dream in real time.

Hunting and fishing in the wilds of Alaska, can only be deemed as paradise, and I was determined to experience it all. But, adventuresome "Cheechakos" (an Alaskan term for rookies) can, and usually do, get themselves into trouble from time to time. I was no exception.

For starters, I insisted on making our annual moose hunts major undertakings, by trekking high up into the mountains instead of hunting just outside Anchorage where we lived. There are moose pretty much every-where in Alaska, but it isn't as big of an adventure in a quick day hunt. I had tried day hunting our first year living in Anchorage and decided it was too tame for me.

I took my two sons, Wayne and Bret, out to the banks of the Little Susitna River near Point McKenzie one day in late September. The weather was beastly warm, all of fifty degrees, and the mosquitoes were out in hoards. Skeeters are so big in Alaska that the FAA makes them put "N" numbers on their wings, trust me!

We did manage to harvest one small bull. We were standing on a small rise on the trail when I heard the telltale sounds of a moose eating aspen branches and walking through the dry underbrush on the other side of a knoll. We had been standing on this little rise overlooking an open muskeg swamp for nearly an hour calling moose and swatting mosquitoes.

Both sides of the trail were heavily wooded with aspen and birch trees and, with the warm and dry weather we had been having, the woods and brittle brush were tough to walk through quietly. I could hear the moose walking, his heavy footsteps going crunch, crunch, as he nonchalantly strolled along on the crisp leaves. It would stop for a bit, probably to munch on some aspens before crunching on once again.

I was certain it was a moose, so I told my oldest son, Wayne, who was sixteen at the time, to quietly crawl, on his hands and knees, up over the knoll and shoot the moose if it was a bull. I decided not to go with him because two people trying to sneak through the noisy underbrush might alarm it. I coached Wayne to be sure to wait for a good broadside shot and aim for the chest cavity just behind the shoulder.

He did an excellent job on his short stalk and nailed the young bull right through the neck at twenty yards. So much for coaching strategy on where to place the shot. It then became a battle between the three of us and about 10 zillion flies and mosquitoes to see who ate the meat. That did it! No more warm weather flatland moose hunting for us. We needed mountains.

That winter I bought maps and topography charts that covered every lick of land within five-hundred miles of Anchorage. After months of research, I selected Tyone Mountain, high up in the Wrangles as my new moose hunting grounds. Getting there was the trick.

The first part of the journey was a three-hundred-mile drive up the Glen Highway to Lake Louise, elevation four-thousand feet. From there we off loaded the eight-wheel-drive, Canadian-built, Argo bush machine and drove it up onto the eighteen-foot Valco Sled riverboat for phase two of the journey. Does this sound like a process? It was.

An Argo is a four-foot-wide by eight-foot-long chunk of hollow plastic, shaped like a bathtub with four wheels on each side. It is chain driven and powered by a two-cylinder, four-stroke Tecumseh engine. Of all the bush machines I had driven in all my years of hunting moose in Canada, this machine performed by far the best in muskeg country.

The Valco Sled was a flat-bottomed riverboat that I had special built by a manufacturer in Seattle, Washington. It had low sides, no seats in the front so as to make room for hauling the Argo and a stand up steering station in the rear. I powered it with a 140 HP Evenrude outboard. For running shallow rivers, I took the lower unit off and replaced the propeller with a bolt-on jet propulsion unit. It was an amazingly fast and fun boat to run rivers in, but for lake running, I left the prop on.

The water part of the journey started at Lake Louise, which is a monstrously large, crystal-clear, body of water several miles across and very deep. It was almost always windswept and full of white-capped waves every time we crossed it. This added more danger to every adventure. Lake Louise was connected to a second lake, Lake Susitna, by a winding and narrow isthmus of water about fifty-yards long.

By contrast, Lake Susitna is nearly fifteen-miles long but only one-mile wide. At the north end of the lake, it narrows down dramatically to form the Tyone River. Approximately five miles down this river, the waterway widens again and turns into Tyone Lake.

The lake is only a couple of miles long and when it narrows down, it becomes the river once again. Tyone Mountain, our final destination, is located another ten miles or so downriver from the Lake. Here the water becomes shallow and fast moving. The Tyone eventually feeds the Susitna River, which runs all the way out to Cook Inlet west of Anchorage. In total, the second phase of our trip measured over forty miles by water.

There is a saddleback between Tyone Mountain and another unnamed mountain to the west that was the last three-mile-long, land course to our final destination. This was flat tundra country north of Tyone Mountain. This was moose hunting paradise, mountains, muskeg, rivers, lakes and many aspen groves for habitat. It was wild and remote. No roads, no cabins and definitely no humans anywhere to be seen. Perfect!

Our first scouting trip to Tyone country was a great adventure. It was early June and the ice was finally off the mountain lakes, so it was time to go check out the terrain that I had mapped out on paper. It was a bright and clear, picture perfect day as we launched the Valco Sled into the clear waters of Lake Louise. This was a recon mission, so we had left the Argo behind. Any land scouting would be on foot.

We found our way across the lakes of Louise, Susitna and Tyone with no trouble and the rest of the voyage down the Tyone River to our landing spot went smooth as well. The water level was high and in no time, we found our saddleback and marked it on out our topographic map.

The next stage in our grand plan was to return in August with the Argo machine and scope out the last leg of the trip in detail, namely create a land trail up and over the saddleback to the muskeg country beyond. Now that I "knew the waterway like the back of my hand," which is Cheechako talk for "I think I know where I am going," I literally flew across the lakes and down the river system, with the Valco Sled up on step all the way, at speeds of thirty to thirty-five mph.

Then, as we rounded the last bend in the river before reaching our docking spot, bam! We hit a submerged boulder with the lower unit of the Evenrude and nearly capsized the boat. We were sent flying through the air sideways, and nearly lost the Argo overboard in the process.

On close examination of the damage, I found that I had knocked a six-inch wide gaping hole in the lower unit just ahead of the propeller. All of the lubricating fluid had been lost in the crash, so there we were forty miles from civilization and with a busted motor. A little afterthought investigation revealed that the water level was at least two feet lower than what it had been when we first came in, right after the ice break-up in June. Massive, close-to-the-surface boulders were now visible everywhere.

An experienced Alaskan would have known that water levels in August would naturally be much lower than in June, and that extreme care would need to be taken when exploring new waterways. This became a big lesson learned for one over-zealous Cheechako. The land scouting would have to wait. We had a problem to solve.

Our only choice was to limp all the way back at idle speed, thus allowing water to lubricate the exposed gears of the lower unit so they wouldn't overheat and lock up. You can do the math. At two mph and over forty miles to go, it took an eternity to get back to our vehicle. We ended up being a day late getting back home, but at least we made it. My wife was fast beginning to get used to wondering where her "boys" were when we went on adventure trips into the very unforgiving Alaska wilderness.

Moose hunting in the mountains of Alaska certainly proved to be much different than hunting their flat land cousins of north central Alberta. That fifty-inch bull that I shot when he charged me was only two and one-half miles from where my brother had live trapped and tagged it four years earlier. The mountain moose of Alaska, on the other hand, are some real vagabonds.

They travel up and down mountain ranges at will. It took a couple of years, but I finally got their patterns figured out.

When in the rut and the weather co-operates, the bulls will definitely be down low with the cows. Find the cows and you will be shooting bulls. When the temperatures are unseasonably warm, go up to the cooler higher elevations to find the bulls.

There is an interesting theory that my brother, the moose biologist and many other experts believe to be true. They believe that although the rutting season for bulls can last several weeks, most of the cows are bred in a three-day period. This happens, they say, so that the bears and wolves cannot kill and devour so many of the calves when they are all born so close together, possibly within 3 days, the next spring. Makes sense, I guess.

*

My son, Bret's first bull was quite an adventure. It all happened on our second year of hunting at Tyone. Our first morning in camp dawned cool and crisp with four inches of fresh snow on the ground. Ideal conditions! I had three hunters in camp, including Bret, and he had drawn the longest straw for the first shot. I led the whole group out in single file toward a little rise in the trail located about three-hundred yards from camp, and between two pothole lakes where I would start making my moose calls.

The wind was calm and I could tell by the emerging light that the day was going to be cloudless.

It was easy to move quietly in the soft snow. I moved the group into position between the two lakes. First, I gave three low-sounding bull grunts and then waited about ten minutes. I always start the call sequence low just in case there is a moose really close by. The second series of calls become increasingly louder and the third is made as loud as possible in order to carry the sound the farthest distance.

I got a strong, quick answer on the second series that morning. I was able to get a quick reading on his location, so I left the other two hunters behind and moved forward about twenty yards with Bret. I gave a couple more grunts and the bull answered immediately. "He's coming in hard," I told Bret, "so get ready!"

I moved us over a bit to our left so that we would have a couple alder bushes for cover. Just then, the young bull, a forty-incher, popped up over the rise in front of us not more than fifty yards away. I coaxed him in even closer with some little moose talk slurps and gurgles.

When the bull was at fifteen yards, I looked over at Bret wondering why he hadn't shot yet. He whispered that his scope was all fogged up and couldn't see a thing, so I handed him the .300 magnum Weatherby and took his old Remington 30-06 from him. He pulled up on the bull, which was kind enough to continue standing there, but all he could see was hair in the scope. I had the 3x9-powered scope dialed all the way up to 9 because I was watching the moose come in and never thought to lower it down again.

The moose was so close and the magnification so high that Bret couldn't make out any specific body parts, only one large blob of brown hair. I give Bret credit for using his head, though. He moved the gun up and to the left to locate the head and antlers, and then back down right again to about where the shoulder should have been before pulling the trigger. The only problem was that as Bret was doing that, the moose was taking one giant step forward at the same time. You guessed it. A gut shot at fifteen yards.

The wounded moose bolted for cover. Bret fired once more and I snapped two quick shots off with Bret's gun while looking alongside the barrel and fogged up scope. We both missed. I told Bret not to worry as we had fresh tracks, a blood trail and plenty of tracking snow so we were sure to catch up to him.

Well, after a couple hours of waiting, sneaking and catching only glimpses of the bull up ahead, our snow cover was melting off fast. The moose was heading downhill, which was a good indicator that he was hit hard, but we were running out of tracking snow, and time.

I asked everyone to strip down to T-shirts and blue jeans in preparation for the race to come. I told every-one, "Here's the plan. I will follow the tracks while running as fast as I can. Bret, you flank me on the right and Wayne and John, you two on my left. Try to stay even with me and keep looking ahead for the bull. Don't worry about making noise because we are not trying to sneak up on him anymore, we are trying to run him down and flush him out."

Off we went on a dead run through the bush. The scant snow cover only lasted for about another half hour, but by then I had seen enough tracks in the snow that I had a pretty good pattern of where the moose was going. I didn't need tracks anymore because I knew that the open and flat muskeg was just ahead of the high ground we were on and I was sure that was where he was headed.

We soon came to a twenty-foot wide stream, but there was no time for hesitation as we all plunged in and waded chest deep through the icy cold water and continued the chase. I caught sight of some fresh hoof prints on the far bank, so I knew we were getting close.

I sprinted on with renewed energy in the direction I thought he would be going, and sure enough finally caught up to him. I was soaking wet from sweat and way ahead of the boys by then, so I finished the bull off with one shot to the heart. Whew, what a race! What a hunt! I was very relieved the moose wouldn't suffer longer, too.

We had run over two miles from where Bret first shot and by now the sun was high and the temperature approaching forty degrees. I sent Wayne back to camp to fetch the Argo while Bret and I field dressed his first bull moose. Bret was sixteen at the time.

A strong bond was formed between my two sons and me through all of our wilderness adventures in Alaska. It is a bond that I am sure, will last forever.

Men truly do discover themselves when faced with danger and adversity and they learn what their hunting companions are made of, too. I am so very proud of the character that my sons possess. They are strong men both physically as well as mentally, fully capable of making good decisions in the wilderness as well as the civilized world. I am very proud to be their father.

Not all of our wilderness adventures were action packed, adrenalin-pumping experiences. We had a lot of relaxing campfire times filled with storytelling and fellowship, too. I remember one moose hunt in particular that was very special.

My oldest son, Wayne and my good friend Bill Mailer accompanied me on a trek into the high country near Denali National Park one year. We made camp one night on a bald topped mountain within sight of Mt. McKinley where the views are nothing short of spectacular. We were above timberline and with our binoculars could easily spot moose, grizzly bears and wolves meandering about the valley floor below us, right up until darkness settled in.

Then, almost as if on cue, the Northern lights appeared directly overhead. It was an amazing display of dancing reds, blues, greens and yellows flashing across the sky. We doused our campfire to gain the full effect and the three of us lay back on the grass to soak it all in. The dazzling lights and the millions of stars out that night seemed so close that we could almost reach out and touch them. We all felt a peace come over us. The serenity was breathtaking. At times like these, one cannot help but realize that the world, and yes the universe, definitely has a creator, an intelligent designer. We all felt closer to our God. His presence was right above us in magnificent splendor.

Bears, Bears and More Bears

I sometimes wonder if a sizable number of the grizzly bears in Alberta Province, Canada, didn't somehow follow me north, when I moved to Alaska. It sure seemed like they did. Maybe it's just that Tom, the "bear magnet" attracts grizzlies no matter what their nationality. Some things never change, I guess, and nearly every hunt at Tyone Mountain involved a grizzly bear encounter of some kind.

At least I had learned some good lessons the hard way down in Canada on how to set up a bear proof tent camp. Well, it wasn't exactly bear proof, but my triangle system at least cut down the danger factor a bit.

The first point of the triangle was the sleep tent. No food is allowed, not even a cracker or piece of pilot bread, only clothes and weapons. The next corner of the triangle, at least fifty feet away, was the cook tent. We had coolers and plastic containers for everything. No food was ever left out exposed to the open air. The last point of the triangle was the trees where the quarters of moose meat would be hung. If bears were to come into camp, they would invariably go to the hanging meat, which was at least fifty feet from the sleeping tent.

The system worked pretty well except for one year when we had one very persistent grizz' come into camp one night. He first showed up about 10:00 p.m. just as we were all getting ready to hit the sack. We could hear him growling and pawing on the trees where the two moose were hanging, so I got out my Smith & Wesson .44 magnum and fired a couple shots in to the air to spook him away.

It worked. He was gone, for about an hour anyway. My two sons and I had to take turns getting up to fire pistol shots in the air every hour almost on the hour 'till daybreak because that bear just would not leave us alone.

The next day I had to load all the meat up on the Argo and take it out of the bush to town. It was either that or move camp, and there was no way we were going to do that. I had this camp set up like the Las Vegas Strip with bright lights hanging everywhere powered by a Honda generator. We had everything but a microwave oven in that camp. It was too comfortable and spiffy for us to move.

On another occasion, I had a big old grizzly wander into camp one day while I was sleeping in the tent. I had been up all night ferrying one group of hunters out and a new batch into camp and needed a quick nap. It had been a thrilling yet exhausting evening of running eighty miles of waterways and six miles of bush country in the dead of night. I put all the hunters on stands and then crashed for a couple hours of much needed rest, only to be awakened by the sound of a grizzly rummaging through our cook tent.

I pulled on boots, grabbed my rifle and burst out of the tent only to trip on a tie-down rope and fall flat on my face. I lay there stunned, helpless in front of this beast, wondering what he would do. The bear, a huge boar grizzly, was obviously surprised. He paused in his rummaging, cocked his head to the side as he stood there looking down on me as if to say *What the hey.* When he saw me pull out the .44 magnum handgun with my left hand and reach out for the rifle with my right, he tore off into the bush before I could get off a shot. Thankfully, he never came back. He was big!

Salmon fishing with grizzly bears presents a whole new set of problems in Alaska. Fishermen versus bear confrontations are common, but usually not tragic because it is the salmon that the bears want to eat, not so much the fishermen. One particular year however, we did have an unusually brave and ornery bear that caused us a lot of trouble.

This particular morning was what Alaska fishermen live for, bright and clear, no wind, *no rain* and temperatures in the low 50's. Perfect! We had been up since 3:00 a.m. My son, Wayne and I had dressed and left his home in Palmer at 3:15 a.m. One quick stop at the local Mac's Steak House in Wasilla (McDonalds'

Restaurants are open 24-7 during the fishing season) for some breakfast-on-the-go and we were on our way up the Parks Highway for the one-hour drive to Montana creek.

The Montana is one of a half dozen clear water streams that form on the western flanks of the Talkeetna Mountain range that flow rapidly to their rendezvous' with the Susitna River. The mighty "Big Su" by contrast is a wide and fast moving body of gray colored silt water, which is fed from the many glaciers that dot the mountaintops of the Talkeetnas.'

By 5:00 a.m. we were fishing on the banks of the Big Su about thirty yards downstream from the confluence of Montana Creek. Here the clear, fresh waters of the Montana hug the shoreline for a couple hundred yards before becoming engulfed by the fast, deep churning gray colored silt waters of the Mighty Susitna.

When salmon run up the glacial river systems of Alaska, they hug the shorelines looking for the clear water streams that are their spawning grounds. When they find clean water at any confluence of a clear water stream, they usually slow down to pause in eddies and drop-offs while they clear their gills, rest and prepare for the next rush upriver.

I was standing on the edge of the bank about twenty feet downstream from Wayne when he looked over at me and said "remember that big ole grizzly bear that we have been seeing every day for the past several days?"

"Yea," I replied, what about him?"

"Well, he is back again and this time is standing about ten feet behind you."

I took a deep breath, gulped hard and immediately slowed the retrieve speed down to a snail's pace. The last thing I needed right then was to hook a salmon and get this bear all excited. By slowing the retrieve, I would be stopping the spinner on the lure from flashing thus making it less noticeable to any salmon that might be nearby.

"What's he doing?" I asked in a rather high pitched and slightly wavering voice.

"Well, he is just sniffing you out right now. Oops! He just took a couple steps closer to you."

I peeked over to my right and saw Wayne slowly reach down with his right hand and unsnap the strap on the holster of his .44 magnum pistol. He gripped the handle and slowly pulled the gun partially free. I could see that he was ready to draw it out the rest of the way if need be. By cocking the hammer in a single motion while drawing the gun, he would be able to quick draw and fire off a shot in a second or less.

Oh great, I thought. *How is he ever going to drop a charging grizzly bear quick-draw cowboy style? I know he is a good shot, but get real—it's my life at stake here!*

Just about everywhere in outdoors Alaska is bear country, so when Wayne and his younger brother Bret reached the age of eighteen, I bought them a Smith & Wesson .44 magnum pistol for their birthday.

A .44 magnum is a powerful weapon, a low caliber elephant gun really, fully able to kill a grizzly bear at close range, but only if, and it is a big if, the shot is placed properly.

My confidence in Wayne grew as I noticed that his hand was not shaking a single twitch as he held it cupped over the handle and firing hammer of his weapon. He was poised and ready to pull and shoot to save his dad from being mauled to death by this ill-tempered ole grizz'.

Wayne kept his cool, not wanting to do anything rash unless he had to, but inside he was shaking like a leaf in the wind. His mind was racing: *Please don't move a muscle, Dad. Please don't get this bear any more upset than he already is. What if he jumps you before I can react with a shot? How do I keep from hitting you instead of the bear? Should I just draw and shoot him now? What if I just wound him? Oh Lord, get us out of this, please!*

At this point, I could hear the bear breathing right behind me. He was huffing and puffing rapidly with short grunts in an excited and agitated manner. I could smell him, too. Yaak, he reeked of dead fish! Grizzly bears are not only carnivorous, they are ravenous scavengers, too, and this ole boy had apparently gotten into some pretty ripe fish carcasses lately. Whew, he stunk!

Then he started growling at me. It was a low-pitched, deep sounding guttural whine of agitation more so than a teeth-gnashing snarl. Yikes, this was unnerving. I could feel the hair on the back of my neck rise and my whole body started to tingle with fear.

In all my wilderness experiences and previous run-ins with bears, nothing was quite as terrifying as being growled at by an angry grizzly bear at a range of eight feet. He was mad, but I was petrified. I was fishing where he wanted to fish and he wanted me gone. I wanted to be gone, too, but he had me cornered up against the river's edge. I was trapped.

We had been watching this troublesome bear for several days and he had never appeared to be particularly dangerous before. If any of us fishermen happened to land a silver salmon or a couple of reds in rapid succession, he would usually amble over to our spot forcing us to depart. Then he'd plunk his fat butt down in the water and take over.

No big deal. He had never growled or charged at any of us before. I guess you could say he bullied us around. The difference this morning, however, was that I had nowhere to retreat. He had me up against the water's edge and the current in this part of the river was too strong and the rushing water too deep for me to escape into. I thought about trying to jump in and swim to safety, but I knew my hip waders would fill with water immediately and pull me under in an instance if I tried it.

Why was he hesitating? Was he confused that a fisherman was actually defying his presence? Did he think that I was standing up to him? Little did he know that I would gladly catch fish and hand feed them to him for a month if he would only let me live.

When I peeked over my shoulder and saw the bear with his ears laid back as he started to sway his head from side to side, all the while popping his lips and pawing the ground, I started to get *really* nervous. These are telltale signs of serious agitation and can mean nothing but trouble when dealing with grizzly bears. I know. I had seen this type of bear behavior many times throughout years of adventures in the great Alaskan and Canadian outdoors.

He was visually upset at my presence and was getting impatient with me. He was going to make a move very soon, I could tell. What would it be? Would he attack or retreat back into the thick bush? I whispered over to Wayne "Get ready, he's gonna make a move."

I could see Wayne loosely holding his fishing pole in his left hand while his right hand was poised and ready to quick-draw and fire his weapon. I was trapped and completely at the mercy of this big grizzly's whim. It was going to take a miracle to get me out of this jam!

"Dear God," I prayed, "If you are out there, I can sure use a little help right now. This bear is going to attack!"

Just then, I happened to look up to see a large salmon leap through the air and splash loudly about forty yards upstream. The bear paused, his attention diverted from me to the fish. When the fish resurfaced and splashed again, the bear took off on the dead run along the bank right past Wayne, almost knocking him over.

Wayne was frantically grabbing at his gun, but was completely disoriented because the bear seemed to be charging him instead of me. His legs shook visibly after the bear sped past him. I couldn't help but to start laughing at the look of shock on Wayne's face as he finally got his pistol drawn. Some cowboy he would make! It took a few seconds before Wayne could appreciate any humor in what had just transpired.

We spotted the bear, a few seconds later, diving into the river near where that noisy salmon had jumped. I think it was a large male silver salmon.

Whew, that was close. I prudently decided to move upstream to fish. Yes Sir! About twenty feet put me elbow to elbow with my new pal Wayne, the man with the *big* handgun.

So, do you think my life was saved by a salmon, or do you think God played a part in that chain of events? Me, I'm definitely leaning toward the God side. There hadn't been a fish surface all morning before that one jumped. In fact, we hadn't had as much as a follow up or hit prior to that. Again, I believe it was divine intervention. I'm definitely not that lucky, no one is.

Encountering grizzly bears and/or black bears while hunting and fishing in Alaska is a pretty normal occurrence. Once you get out of the city limits of Anchorage, there are always adventures waiting to happen. I can't count how many times I've had bears growling at me from the underbrush when I have been out hunting moose near my cabin in the Talkeetna Bluffs. They just always seem to be around me wherever I go. So, a few years ago I decided to buy a grizzly bear tag and hunt *them* for a change.

Late August and September is berry eating time for bears, and the ten-mile-long trail leading from Talkeetna to the cabin in Talkeetna Bluffs is chuck full of them at that time of year. Bears love wild blueberries, current berries, crowberries, and the high bush cranberries that grow along the trails. In addition, the many clear water streams that flow from countless high mountain lakes are filled with spawning red, silver and pink salmon, which makes this part of Alaska, in the fall, a veritable smorgasbord for bears.

Autumn is also one of the most beautiful times of the year in the foothills of the Talkeetnas'. By mid-August, the birch and aspen leaves have turned to a brilliant yellow and orange, and the alder groves are a deep brown, almost rust in color. The ever-present fireweed plants are a brilliant red and the devil's clubs have turned almost black with their masses of prickly thorns loose and ready to inflict pain on any unsus-pecting person that might get close enough to touch one of them.

From several of the high points along the trail, one can look north and see the snow-covered peaks of Mt McKinley in its entire splendor, provided the top few thousand feet aren't covered in a bank of clouds, that is. Mt. McKinley is so high, over twenty thousand feet, that it creates its own weather and often surrounds it-self in clouds.

As I left the cabin early that fall morning, and started to hunt down the Talkeetna Trail, I couldn't help but to marvel anew at the beauty of the bluffs. Cool crisp air, a thin layer of frost on the ground, au-tumn colors brilliantly displayed on the foliage, and *bear tracks everywhere*. Black bears as well as griz-zlies were working the streams and berry patches along the trail in great numbers. It was hard to walk more than fifty yards without crossing a fresh bear track in the muddy trail.

It is somewhat unusual for black bears to cohabi-tate with grizzlies because grizzlies have been known to attack and kill their much smaller cousins from time to time, but the rich food sources of the area bring both species in for a more peaceful feast. There was so much food the two species didn't bother each other.

After walking the trail for about two hours, while looking and listening intently from side to side, I final-ly heard the telltale sound of a grizzly bear's presence, the crashing down of a dead tree. No other animal in the bush purposely knocks down trees, only grizzlies looking for grubs or ground squirrels.

I happened to be on top of a little knoll at the time and the bear was approximately sixty yards off to my right. The thick brush was over five-feet tall and the slight breeze was blowing from the bear toward me, so all conditions for a stalk were perfect. I hunched lower to the ground and slowly crept up to within forty yards of him.

About this time, I wished I'd had a bow and arrows for a weapon instead of a rifle because I knew that I could very easily get to within ten to fifteen yards, which would make for an ideal archery shot.

As it was, forty yards was amply close for a good killing shot with the rifle. I waited until the grizz' turned, allowing for a rear-quartering angle shot and squeezed off one round with a .300 magnum Weatherby. I nailed him in the heart and right lung dropping him like a ton of bricks. One and done, my short hunt was over.

The grizzly measured eight-feet-six-inches from nose to tail and the same from claw to claw. It was not the largest interior grizzle bear ever taken, but certainly a respectable trophy from which to make a bearskin rug, which I did. The best part? I didn't need any miracles to survive the experience. That was a real bonus

Fishing Alaska

Fishing the five species of salmon that frequent the rivers and streams of Southcentral Alaska provided numerous adventures for us as a family. My wife and daughter enjoyed it as much as the boys and I did, unless there was too much adventure involved, that is.

My daughter, Kelly Jo actually caught the largest king salmon ever caught by any of us. When she turned sixteen years old, I took her on a trip to Soldotna to fish the Kenai River. It was just Father and Daughter off on an adventure together. It was great.

Although I usually hated fishing the Kenai because it had so blasted many tourists on it, I really wanted "K.J." to catch a nice king. It didn't take long, either. On our third or fourth drift past Eagle Rock, she hooked into a monster 64-pound, 46-inch, king salmon. After a tough but fairly short battle, as we continued drifting down river, I netted her trophy king salmon for her and we stopped for the day. What a memorable adventure it was. I had that fish mounted for her so that neither one of us would ever forget the experience.

As it was with our hunting adventures, day trips for fishing were far too boring for me. We needed to get further out from civilization and challenge the wilderness, and believe me, challenge it we did.

For several years, our favorite weekend getaway was to leave Anchorage on Friday night after work and trailer the Valco Sled boat 125 miles to a boat landing on the Susitna River near the town of Talkeetna. From there it was a forty-mile jaunt down the "Big Su" to the confluence of Deshka Creek where the king and silver salmon runs were spectacular.

We spent the weekends camping and fishing before returning back upriver on Sunday nights. Every trip was an adventure, whether fighting strong currents and floating debris to chasing bears out of camp at night. Yes, the bear magnet even attracted grizzlies on fishing trips.

The Little Susitna River has one of the greatest runs of silver salmon as any river in Alaska, and silvers are, pound for pound, the greatest fighters of them all. Access to the mouth of the Little Su where it empties into Cook Inlet can be either a major challenge, or simply a very long trip, depending on which approach you take. The safest and most logical choice is to take the long trip up the Parks highway to Wasilla, which, by the way, is "all I saw," spelled backward.

Some of the early Alaskans definitely had a sense of humor when it came to naming their towns. Take the example of Chicken, Alaska. It was named such because the miners that founded the little town didn't know how to spell Ptarmigan, which is the state bird. Oh well, at least the next town up the road from Chicken was aptly named Eagle.

At Wasilla, we'd off-load the boat at a public landing and then spend several hours at agonizingly slow speeds navigating the narrow, slow-moving and winding twenty-mile long waterway down to the confluence with Cook Inlet. Oh, there were plenty of spots to fish for silvers all along the Little Su, but at the mouth was where the real action was.

When salmon first enter freshwater streams and rivers from the saltwater oceans, they are bright silver in color and at their most energetic state. The more time they spend in fresh water the redder in color they become and the slower they move as their bodies begin to change shape. They are actually beginning to die at that stage. Besides, there is no adventure in a day trip, you know. For these reasons, plus the fact that not many people were willing to venture all the way to the confluence of Cook Inlet, it was precisely why it appealed so much to us.

After several slow, but safe trips downriver to our fishing spot through the years, it became apparent that a faster, more adventuresome route needed to be taken. Crossing the open ocean waters of Cook Inlet was the answer. The challenges of such a venture were many, however.

The number one concern was the tides, which are some of the most radical in the world. Their average is over twenty-eight feet, which at low tide converts Cook Inlet into a veritable mud flat for as far as the eye can see, well past the mouth of the Little Su some forty miles out. Then, twelve hours later, the entire Inlet would be under several feet of water. The incoming and out-going water could reach speeds upwards of thirty mph, which was also a major concern. Wind conditions and the potential for rough seas had to be taken into account as well.

After much research and planning, we were finally ready for our first attempt at crossing the inlet. The plan was for me, and my two sons, Wayne and Bret, to depart the Port of Anchorage right at high tide so that we would be riding the receding tide out while it was at its slowest speed as we headed west. The mouth of the Little Susitna River was on the north shore and well marked by a buoy we were told. The return trip two days later would be the same process, only in reverse.

The trip out was great! Sunny skies, no wind, calm seas and a well-marked buoy provided for an ideal first time experience of crossing the inlet. We motored up-river about three miles and anchored at our usual fishing hole, just as the first wave of silvers came through.

Salmon ride the high tides into the rivers of Alaska, and where we anchored, we were close enough to Cook Inlet that the current of the little Su would actually slow, stop and then reverse direction as the tide overpowered the river's current.

At the next ebb, when the river was about to start flowing again, is when the silvers would show up en masse. We hooked and caught those tail-walking maniacs as fast we could reel them in for the next hour. After that, the pace slackened a bit, but the fishing was still good for a couple more hours before that particular run would be over. What a blast!

By late Sunday afternoon after limiting out on silvers for two days running, it was time to catch the next high tide and head back across the inlet to Anchorage. I timed our departure so that we were coming out of the river and into the inlet approximately one hour before peak high tide—which was exactly the very wrong thing to do.

Little did I realize that this particular tide was a good eight feet lower than the high tide that we came over on and that the mud flats at the mouth of the river were only be about six inches below water level. Oops.

We didn't get more than a couple hundred yards into the inlet before we came to a slithering halt, miring ourselves into the muck of the mud flats. We were beached. *Now what?* I thought. For a few minutes, I was at a loss to explain what had happened, but as the high tide slackened and the water started to recede, my error in judgment became apparent.

We discovered that the riverbed, which was still running strongly, was about one-hundred yards away. The error also provided the future solution: don't leave this river to enter the inlet at any time less than two hours either side of high tide or you won't be able to tell where the mud flats meets the riverbed.

Soooo, what do we do now? I checked the tide book only to learn that the next high tide high enough to float us off the mud flats wouldn't be coming for another week!

I said, "Okay, boys. Let's unload the boat, hook a rope to the bow and tow it over to the riverbed." What a job that was, but we had no choice. Fortunately, I had two strong backs beside my own that were up to the task.

By the time we got to the riverbed, it was a good ten feet below the top of the mud flats we were on, so we simply slid the eighteen-foot Valco down the bank, reloaded all our equipment and waited twelve hours for the next high tide.

We got home late that Sunday night, but at least we got home safe and sound, with another lesson well learned on how to survive in the wilds of Alaska.

Miracle At Sea

Through the years, we made several trips across Cook Inlet to fish the mouth of the Little Susitna River. These trips were not without risk, however. The seas off the coast of Anchorage can become perilous at times. I recall reading many accounts of small craft, caught up in sudden storms, where all lives were lost after their boats swamped during high seas, or they crashed onto the rocks on the north shore of the Inlet.

Anchorage is located on a point of land that juts out into Cook Inlet. Approximately ten miles due west of the city is an uninhabited twenty acre island named Fire Island. On both sides of the Anchorage "point," are large bays called Arms. Turnagain Arm extends southeastward a good fifty miles and ends at Portage Glacier. Knick Arm stretches northeasterly for about thirty miles and is fed by two glaciers, the Knick Glacier and the Matanuska. Windstorms often develop without warning off these glaciers and turn once calm seas into tempests of peril.

Bill Mailer had become one of my best hunting and fishing partners through the years. His daughter and my Kelly Jo were teammates on the high school swim team. I knew Bill was *my kind of sportsman* the first time we hunted together when I saw him stoop down to pick up a candy wrapper that some other hunter had discarded along the trail. We both cared immensely about the environment and the unmatched beauty of Alaska is so well worth preserving.

On one particular Friday afternoon in late June, Bill called to say that he had just heard that a new run of silver salmon were beginning to enter the Little Su and wanted to know if the boys and I were up for an inlet crossing. Silly question. We checked our tide books and decided to meet at the Port of Anchorage at 9:00 a.m. the next morning.

Our normal procedure whenever the four of us were fishing together, was to take 2 boats, his 19-foot Gregor, powered by a 90-HP, Evenrude outboard, and my 21-foot Duckworth, powered by a .351 CID-Ford inboard. My oldest son, Wayne usually rode with Bill.

After launching our boats that morning, I checked in for the weather report on my ship-to-shore radio. Winds were out of the southeast at fifteen knots and the seas were two feet, not ideal conditions, but manageable we thought. The high tide was nearing, so we fired up our engines and headed out to sea for the one and one-half hour voyage west.

We hadn't been gone two minutes, before Bill's engine quit running. "Some sort of electrical problem" Bill informed me over the radio. I watched him go to the rear of his boat and bang on his battery box a couple times before firing the engine again. A few knocks always work, so off we went running side by side for another four or five minutes before the engine quit again.

This happened over and over again with the same result, Bill tinkering, banging or kicking his cable connections, the engine re-firing and then running for just a few more minutes. After nearly an hour of these constant delays, the winds started to pick up and the seas had risen close to four feet. We were over half way to the confluence of the Little Su and basically smack dab in the middle of Cook Inlet, well past Fire Island.

"We need to get a move on, Bill," I radioed, so we both hit the throttles and sped off as fast as we could, but the wind and waves started to overwhelm us. It was what I feared most—a sudden windstorm off Portage Glacier had us in its grip.

After a few minutes, Bill radioed, "I can't make it, Tom. The waves are coming in over my stern" Bill's boat was lower and smaller than mine was and the waves were coming directly behind us. He was slowly being swamped.

"Let's turn back, then. We will run a quartering angle into the waves at a northeast heading. Try to power up the waves and pull back on your throttle once you crest the tops." I answered. "I'll run with you." My boat was much faster and I was not experiencing the same problems, but I wasn't about to abandon Bill and Wayne.

Within minutes, the waves reached twenty feet at the crest with no sign of letting up. Looking at the north shore, I could see that we were getting steadily pushed in that direction by the ever-increasing wind and waves. This was not good.

The shallow water along that rocky shoreline was exactly where many boats and crews had perished in years past. "We have to go faster, Bill," I yelled into the radio. "Pour it on for all you are worth! Take a more easterly tack and nail that throttle to the firewall!"

I looked over to the right and shuddered with fear as I saw Bill and my son, Wayne hanging on for dear life as their boat went flying up and off the crest of a forty-foot wave and going completely airborne before slamming into the next wave with the bow pointed straight downward.

"I don't think they are going to make it." I said to my son, Bret. "If they get sideways to the waves, they are sure to go over." Every wave coming now is a "forty footer." I was also struggling to keep my boat upright.

The navigating technique Bill and I were using was to "power up" each wave in an easterly direction at full throttle. Once we reached the crest and could feel that we were going airborne, we cut the throttle before our propellers left the water and prepared for the ensuing crash as we slammed down onto the back-side of that wave and watched the bow of our boats disappear alarmingly under the water of the next wave. As soon as the buoyancy of the bow, thankfully, caused it to "pop" back up, we hit the throttle wide open again to drive up the next wave.

We repeated this procedure over and over, again and again, as we battled the raging sea. One time the boat slammed down so hard off a wave crest, that the radio was ripped off its mounts on the cabin ceiling. We were hanging on for dear life as we were being banged about in our fragile little craft. I was afraid that any second Bill's engine would quit and leave him and Wayne helpless.

"Bret, we need to agree to something." I yelled over the roar of the storm. "If they capsize, we have to try to rescue them, even if it means that we capsize as well. If this happens, we will all most likely be killed. If we don't drown, we will most assuredly be crushed into the rocks on the north shore."

"I know, Dad. I've been thinking the same thing" he replied, "We have to try, no matter what. I'm with you." So, we agreed. Today might be the day that we both died and we both knew it, but we would not ab-andon Wayne and Bill.

We were in a frantic battle with the elements and we were losing. The rocky north shore was looming closer and closer and I mentally began to prepare for the worst. Just then, I began to notice, hopefully, that the last few waves were a little smaller than the previous ones.

Could it be? Or was this just wishful thinking? *Yes, I was sure of it!* I looked off to the south and sure enough, there was Fire Island off in the distance. We had reached the leeward side of Fire Island, which was breaking the wind for us. We were going to make it!

We gradually started making steady headway toward the Port of Anchorage and the waves continued to diminish in size. Forty-five minutes later, when we got back to port, the seas were a manageable three to four feet. Then, just as we pulled in to the dock, *Bill's engine quit running*. We all looked at each other in total silence.

That engine had not run any more than five to ten minutes straight at any time until the storm hit. Then it held on nonstop for nearly an hour and a half as we battled our way back to safety. Had Bill's engine quit running any time during the storm, Bill and Wayne would have immediately capsized and been lost at sea. Bret and I would have tried to save them, but our odds of capsizing and perishing with them would have been nearly 100 percent.

It was a miracle, and we all knew it. It was a miracle that we made it even with the engine *running*. Just one twist or turn the wrong way and that boat would have foundered and been flipped by the waves.

It was beyond miraculous that Bill's engine had somehow kept running for so long at the most critical time.

We tied up our boats and hugged each other in near tears. God had saved us from certain death.

All of us were deeply affected by this harrowing experience. None of us ever talked about it much, but then again none of us ever attempted another Cook Inlet crossing, either.

I really think the Cook Inlet incident was the closest I have ever come to death. The battle with the high seas lasted nearly one and a half hours, so I had plenty of time to experience real fear. The lives of my two sons and my good friend, Bill were at stake besides my own, and that fact was especially sobering to me.

Most of the other life-saving miracles that God had provided me were personal, quick nanosecond changes of fate that left no time for contemplation. This miracle moved me deeply.

"Why did you save my life again, Lord? Was it just to save Bill and the boys, or am I just as important as them in your eyes? I am not worthy, God. I know that I am not, but thank you for saving Wayne, Bret and Bill. Thank you!"

Big Mac Publishers

The Great Dahl Sheep Adventure

Having graduated from "Cheechako" status through several years of Alaska outdoor adventures only meant that I prepared myself better for trips into the wilderness than I did before. The "Cavalier Canadian" outlook on adventure had ended. Alaska is too wild and unforgiving not to take the utmost care in preparation for every trip. That doesn't mean that the danger and daring were over, though. No way! We just became smarter and better prepared for our near death experiences.

Our Dahl sheep hunt of 1984 tested every bit of wilderness skills and savvy that I had gained through the years. It tested the metal of everyone on that trip with me, too. This was to be our most adventurous undertaking ever!

Dahl sheep live in the high country of many of the mountain ranges in Alaska. They are beautiful animals with bright white fur and massive horns that flair outward from their heads as they curl. Conversely, Rocky

Mountain Big Horn Sheep, native only to the Rocky Mountains, are browner in color and with horns that curl in close to their heads. Both make spectacular mounts, but the Dahl is considered by many to be the most special to behold.

Our chosen hunting grounds was the Nabesna Glacier country, high up in the Wrangle Mountains, located 150 miles south of Tok, Alaska and 100 miles due west of the Canadian border.

Most sheep hunting in this area is done by utilizing bush planes to fly into the remote wilderness and land above timberlines on bald mountaintops near where Dahl sheep have been spotted. Our plan was more adventuresome than that. It entailed the use of four-wheel-drive trucks, eight-wheeled-drive, all-terrain vehicles, boats, floatation devices, motors, hip waders and an abundance of ropes. Tons of imagination was needed, too.

On August 7, the trip began with a three-hundred-mile drive from Anchorage, up the Glenn Highway, to Slana on the Tok Cut Off road. What followed then was a fifty-mile jaunt down a dirt/gravel road that dead-ended at the old abandoned gold mine at Nabesna.

This old mining site, our point of debarkation, was in full view of the Nabesna Glacier, which was off to the east some five miles away. I am reasonably sure that the rest of the journey that I had mapped out for us, was the first such trip ever attempted by man, and probably for good reason.

We first loaded up the eight-wheel drive Argo ATV with all our gear and equipment then top loaded that with a twelve foot inflatable rubber boat and a 10 HP outboard motor. With me driving the Argo, and my four companions, Wayne, Bret, my brother, Gerry and his son Mark walking, we blazed a five-mile-long trail down to the Nabesna River. We had to cross two fairly wide streams in the process, but we had a technique pre-established for this.

Knowing that the Argo was amphibious, albeit not very stable in open water, I had attached a Styrofoam collar all around the perimeter of the machine to gain buoyancy and stability. When we got to a river, my four companions put on their chest waders and crossed the streams ahead of me, dragging a tow rope along as they went, leaving one end of the rope tied to the ATV. Once they reached the far side, I would drive the ATV into the water and they would pull me across with the tow rope. It worked amazingly well, I must say.

However, when we reached the banks of the Nabesna, a much larger river, we had to change tactics somewhat, but we were prepared for that as well.

I knew that the waters of the river were deeper, the current stronger and the color of the water a silty gray due to being glacier fed. This would make it impossible to see the bottom. The river was also very wide, at least a mile across, and full of gravel bars that gave the river a braided look with no less than a dozen different channels to cross.

This is where the inflatable Zodiac boat and the outboard motor came into play. The boys motored across each channel dragging the tow rope behind the Zodiac boat, again leaving one end tied to the ATV. I simply drove the ATV into the water letting the current swing me to the other side as the guys held on to the rope. It was much more difficult to keep the machine upright in the stronger currents of the river, but that was all part of the adventure.

We eventually made it all the way across the river with no major complications. Whew, the worst was over, or so we thought. We still had to travel five miles downriver before intersecting with Stone Creek and then another ten-mile trip up the Stone Creek watershed to the stream's headwaters.

The topography maps that I had purchased showed a trail running through the bush all the way to Stone Creek. Unfortunately, these maps were thirty years old and not a trace of such a trail remained. So, we blazed our own trail through the alder patches and aspen groves, which took an entire day in itself. Much to our delight, the Stone Creek watershed held no surprises and matched our maps.

Typical of most mountain streambeds, this watershed terrain was about two-hundred yards wide, full of gravel with only a narrow stream of water flowing through it. During spring break-up, however, the entire watershed area would be a raging torrent of water flowing from the headwaters in a downhill rush to the Nabesna River below.

The trip up Stone Creek was uneventful and that a pleasant experience. The weather had been great for three days and we were exploring new territory. We were quite possibly the first humans ever to walk this particular land and that made it even more exiting and special.

When we finally reached the headwaters, a flat plateau at nearly six thousand feet elevation, we were only a few hundred feet below timberline. This wooded plateau was roughly two and one-half miles wide and it was completely surrounded by mountain peaks on three sides. All the spring run-off from near-by mountain streams emptied into this plateau forming Stone Creek, which in turn flowed ten miles westward down to the Nabesna River.

I selected a thick spruce grove, well protected from the wind, for our campsite. By the time we got our tents set up and camp put in order, it was getting late in the day, too late to set out scouting, so we grabbed our two spotting scopes to check out the surrounding slopes. Much to our delight, we spotted no less than six legal rams (three-quarter curl minimum) right from camp. We were pumped! This was going to be a hunt to remember.

The next day, August 10, was the opening day of sheep hunting in Alaska, and it couldn't have been more perfect weather wise. The sun didn't rise over the mountaintops 'till well after 7:00 a.m. but when it did, it shone brightly without a cloud in the sky. Our plan was simple. My brother, Gerry would take his son, Mark and head down stream to hunt and I would take my two sons, Wayne and Bret and head upstream. Beyond that, we didn't have anything specific planned.

None of us had ever hunted Dahl sheep before, so we had to figure out how to go about it as we went along. I dug out a spotting scope and glassed the rocky slopes, but no sheep were to be seen. Then, I must have slipped into a state of delusional *Cheechakoism* by deciding we should actually climb up a mountain to see what we could see.

Well, we climbed the highest peak that was available, only to dead end at a rock cliff near the top, with no place to go except back down again. "Boy, that was dumb" I had to admit. So, we climbed back down, this time on a quartering angle to the creek below which put us nearly a mile upstream from camp, once we reached the valley floor.

Once there, I noticed one important thing. There were an unusually large number of grizzly bear tracks all over the place. Years ago I had come up with a new name for Alaska grizzlies, "RBLTLs," which means really big long toothed lads, not just LTLs, like we used to call their much smaller cousins that live in

Canada. *Could I not ever go into the wilderness without finding grizzly bears in abundance?*

I noticed an inviting little grassy knoll on the other side of Stone Creek that looked like a perfect spot to rest, and do some more glassing for sheep, so I waded across and climbed to the top of it. When I turned back, I found that neither Wayne nor Bret had followed my lead. "Hey, what's up guys?" I asked. "C'mon over, it's nice up here."

Neither one of the boys would budge. They already had blisters on their feet and had no interest in getting their feet wet and making matters worse. After all, they had *walked* the twenty miles up the mountain to the camp, while I had *driven* the Argo.

By now, the sun was shining brightly and the temperature was about fifty degrees. I took my shoes and socks off and laid them out to dry on the grass. That was enough to coax Bret to join me, but not Wayne. He was too stubborn, and probably too smart as well.

After about twenty minutes of glassing the mountain slopes, I spotted what appeared to be a full curl ram about a mile away, high up on the slope of a mountain, next to the one we had just descended. It was on Wayne's side of Stone Creek, so I devised a plan of attack and went down to where Wayne was resting on the stream bank to talk it over.

He did the stalking and I stood where I could see both he and the ram. I used hand signals to direct him. If I held my arm straight up it meant for him to climb higher. Pointing my arm laterally meant for him to move in the direction that I was pointing. I used the spotting scope to monitor the ram and he used the scope on his rifle to watch me.

I don't know if this technique was a common way to hunt sheep or not, but we were going to try it just the same.

The terrain at this elevation was mostly barren rock except where the ravines were located. They were filled with vegetation comprised mostly of small trees and brush. The ram was feeding on some of that brush high up in a ravine about a quarter mile above Wayne and close to a mile off to his right.

The plan actually worked pretty well. It took nearly an hour, but the ram stayed put and I directed Wayne almost right to it. When he reached the ravine he was about two-hundred yards below the ram, so his uphill shot was a bit off, just wounding it.

The ram ran off and disappeared over a rock ledge, and we watched as Wayne climbed up and over that ledge and disappeared from our sight. There was Bret and I, wondering what happened and where Wayne had gone. The suspense was killing us, so after about fifteen or twenty minutes, Bret couldn't take it. He just had to climb up the mountain and help his brother.

I provided the same directional guidance for Bret as I had done for Wayne and soon, both of my sons were up a mountain, over a ledge and out of sight.

It wasn't long after Bret disappeared, that I got too antsy and couldn't wait any longer, so I also headed up the mountain. It took me nearly an hour to scale the rock shale area in order to come out just below where I had last seen Bret, but I was off a little and found myself up against a vertical rock ledge that I couldn't climb. I tried calling loudly to them. Fifteen minutes later, Bret appeared about twenty feet above me, on top of the ledge and told me what was going on.

Wayne had caught up to the ram near the peak of the mountain and finished it off with one shot. Unfortunately, the ram had fallen down into a steep rock lined ravine, so he climbed down after it. After skinning, quartering and tying it all onto his backpack, he soon discovered that he couldn't possibly pack all that unbalanced weight on his shoulders and make it back up and out of the ravine. He was stuck!

I dug out a section of rope that I had with me and handed it, along with my belt, up to Bret and told him that Wayne should tie everything all of us could possibly scrape together, to make the longest rope possible and try to hoist the load out of the ravine.

Well, Bret came back a little later and told me that the rope he had pieced together was still too short and Wayne was still stuck down in that ravine. I looked at my watch, then at the fading sun and told Bret to tell Wayne that it is now or never. "Either he packs that ram up out of that ravine right now or he leaves it behind and comes out alone."

It was getting late in the day and we still had two miles to travel in unfamiliar grizzly country to get back to camp. A few minutes later, both boys appeared above me with the Dahl sheep intact on the pack.

Wayne told me later that strapping that heavy pack on his back and crawling vertically up those slippery rocks was the scariest thing he had ever done, but there was no way he was going to leave his trophy 1¼-curl ram behind.

A half hour later, we were back down off the mountain and on the banks of Stone Creek. We still had a two-mile hike ahead of us and daylight was fading fast. "Guys, we have a problem." I said. "It is almost dark and we are two miles from camp. There is no trail to follow and there is grizzly sign everywhere. I'm not sure we can find the campsite once we get close because it is fifty yards or so from the streambed, off in the trees and it will be pitch dark long before then. We could possibly walk right past it."

Wayne proved once again to me that he is a man that I can always rely upon. "Dad, you take the flashlight and your rifle and lead us out of here, okay? You just shoot the bears and find the camp. Bret and I will be right behind you with the rest of the gear and equipment. Don't worry about us."

With that said, he hoisted the eighty-pound backpack with the sheep on it, put it on his back, and told Bret to grab the rest, which was two rifles, another empty backpack and the warm coats we had all worn in the morning. Off we went.

I stopped a couple times to see if anyone needed to rest, but Wayne simply said, "I've got this pack on my back and it's not coming off 'till we reach camp." Wayne is a mountain of a man at six-foot-four and solid muscle. His brother, Bret is no slouch either at six-foot-two and is as strong as a bull.

On we trudged, following the streambed on a moonless night with only a small flashlight to find the way. There is no doubt in my mind that we would have walked right past our campsite and continued down the valley if it were not for my brother, Gerry saving the day for us.

You see, he and his son Mark had bagged a nice full curl ram that morning and had been hanging around camp all afternoon waiting for us to return. When it got dark and we weren't back yet, he figured we might need a little help finding our way so he took a Coleman lantern out to the streambed and left it there on the bank all lit up for me to find. He figured that I would be following the streambed on the way down the valley, and he was right.

Through the many years of moose hunting with him in Canada, we had eerily begun thinking alike when out in the bush. Once we found the lantern, it was easy to find our campsite. We had made it! One big adventure was over, but it wouldn't be the last one for this trip.

What a spectacular first day of hunting this had been. Two hunts and two legal rams in camp. Gerry and Mark's hunt had been easier than ours. They did it the correct way by glassing the slopes from the valley floor *first*. After spotting a ram on the mountainside that would be within a reasonable range for stalking, they climbed up after it, being careful to stay hidden until they were close enough for a shot. One shot from less than two-hundred yards and Mark had his first Dahl sheep. By two in the afternoon, they had the meat processed and were back in camp relaxing and wondering what we were up to.

The next morning, day 2 of the hunt and day 5 of the adventure, we awoke to a steady rainfall, so all hunting was put on hold. The wet and rocky slopes were too slippery for us to climb. Final cleaning up of the two ram capes and a cribbage tournament made up the day's activities.

The third day in camp, August 12, we awoke to six inches of fresh snow on the ground. *Yikes, what did we get ourselves into?* I thought. The temps didn't seem that cold, so we waited out the day to see if it would warm up and melt the snow so we could get back to hunting. Gerry and I were both getting a little uneasy knowing that we were seventy miles from the nearest civilization with no contact to the outside world whatsoever and it was snowing.

The next morning, day 4, heightened our fears even more as another ten inches of snow had fallen.

The wind had picked up and the temperature had dropped significantly. We were in a blizzard at six-thousand feet in the Wrangle Mountains on August 13. It was time to get ourselves off that mountain as fast as we could. We had two streams and the Nabesna River to cross, plus twenty miles of trail to find and follow just to get back to our vehicles.

We loaded up the Argo, leaving whatever we could behind to lighten the load, and broke camp by mid-morning. It was a struggle fighting through the snow but at least we were going downhill. It took us the rest of that day just to reach our crossing spot on the Nabesna River, and what a shock we found when we got there that afternoon.

At this lower elevation, most of the precipitation for the last several days had been in the form of rain rather than snow and the river was nothing less than a raging torrent of water coming down off the glacier just five miles upriver. Instead of only one river channel being deep and fast running, they all were.

There were twelve in all, separated by gravel bars that were nearly submerged. This was not good. It was nearly dark by then, so we decided to make camp on the riverbank and tackle the crossing the next morning. We were hoping conditions would improve overnight.

The next day was worse. Our final quest to reach safety turned into our biggest test for survival. The temperature had dropped into the low twenties and we were in a white- out condition with the snow flying horizontally, churned along by the fifty mph winds being whipped up off the glacier.

My brother and I surveyed the situation as we paced up and down the shoreline trying to find our best chances for a smooth crossing. There were none.

We thought of delaying the attempt and trying to wait out the storm, but that was not a viable option. Conditions could get worse instead of better and our food supply was getting perilously low.

I called the three boys and my brother together to go over a plan. "We will need the boat and motor for each of the twelve channels we have to cross because the water is too deep and fast to wade across. All four of you guys go across in the boat together while I hold on to my end of the tow rope. Once you are across and have the rope taut, be ready to walk me down the river as you hold the rope because the strong current will not allow me to simply drive into the water and swing myself across like we did when we came in. I cleared out the entire front section of the Argo so that I can maneuver myself around quickly to keep the machine balanced."

We had also lost most of our Styrofoam floatation devices while blazing the trail down to Stone Creek, so I knew the machine would not be very stable in the water. "So, are you guys ready? This is survival time. We must get across this river in order to get to safety. We have no choice in the matter. Be careful. Be strong. Let's go!"

The first channel crossing nearly ended in disaster. Once I drove the machine into the current, I was swept downriver so fast that I almost tipped over. I took on a lot of water as I frantically scrambled to regain balance.

This was not going to be easy. After draining out the machine, once we landed it safely on the first gravel bar it was time to challenge the next channel and the next channel, and the next. There were eleven before we approached the last and widest one. By this time it was getting very late in the day. We were all soaking wet and freezing cold. The wind and driving snow had been relentless the entire day.

We were exhausted and that last channel was so wide and the current so strong that we were very disheartened and discouraged. I was beginning to worry about whether our group was going to make it, so I made the decision to abandon the Argo machine on the last gravel bar and boat everyone across. I felt I had to get everybody warmed up and dried out before hypothermia set in. The situation was that desperate. The three boys were beginning to shake badly from the cold as they sat huddled up on the ground using the ATV as a windbreak.

With the decision having been made, we made two trips across the last channel to get the rest of our equipment on solid ground and while the boys set up our tent Gerry and I built a campfire—a big hot raging campfire.

By this time, darkness had set in and I realized that I had made the right decision. We needed rest and nourishment to get us through one more day of our struggle to survive and reach safety. I hated to leave the machine sitting on that wide-open gravel bar overnight fearing the river might rise and sweep it away. If that were to happen, we would not have the Argo to carry the boat and equipment. We would need to drag our Zodiac boat by hand for four miles through the wilderness. We needed the Zodiac to have a way to cross the two streams that were still between our vehicles and us. The vehicles were parked at the Nabesna mine. I knew that with the heavy rain those two streams would be too wide and too deep to wade across.

That evening we ate pilot bread and spreadables again, since the rest of our food supply had been depleted a couple days earlier. Pilot bread is nothing more than a very large circular shaped soda cracker and spreadables are little tubes of different types of meats and veggies that you can squeeze out for sandwich spreads.

Once the five of us were fed, warmed and dry, we collapsed into our sleeping bags and fell fast asleep instantly.

"What a day of endurance this had been. I was so proud of my two boys and Gerry's son, Mark for their stamina and courage. We had been in a very dangerous situation all day long fighting the elements. On more than one occasion, several of them lost footing and nearly were pulled into the raging river current. Nevertheless, everyone helped out and stood by each other for nearly ten hours through that freezing blizzard. We were not out of danger yet, but at least we were on dry ground on the homeward side of the Nabesna River. Come what may tomorrow, at least we were safe for one more night.

The next day dawned clear and sunny. The storm had ended and our spirits were high as we looked across that last river channel at the ATV machine still parked on the gravel bar where I had left it.

"Halleluiah, praise the Lord! We just might make it out of here yet," sang my brother, Gerry.

However, the task of getting that machine to dry land was going to be a daunting one. The river had risen overnight. The current was faster and I wasn't sure that we had enough rope to stretch across the width of the channel, which at this point was nearly seventy-yards wide.

It was close, but we had barely enough rope. My brother and the boys talked me out of trying to ride the machine across the channel and I'm glad they did. The current was raging!

My revised plan was this. I drove the machine right up to the water's edge on the gravel bar and left it in neutral gear with the tow rope attached to the front of it. I motored across to the other shore carrying the tow rope. Once there, the five of us planned to slowly pull the Argo via the tow rope into the current and guide it across.

If it worked, we'd load our gear back into the Argo and be merrily on our way home. Right? Wrong. We ran into a major problem once we got the machine about half way across.

The current in the middle was so strong that as we held the tow rope the front of the machine was being pulled under water. We tried to counter this by running along the shore, with the current, to ease the tension in the rope so that the machine would resurface and float once again and that worked fine, well, for a while at least.

Two-hundred yards down the shoreline, we came to a large stand of aspen trees at the water's edge, thus blocking the rope and our path. When the machine and our group reached the trees, the tow line drew taut and down went the machine under water again.

"Let her go!" I yelled out. "We will have to run it down and hope that it gets caught up in a gravel bar somewhere down river."

As soon as the tension on the rope loosened, the ATV resurfaced and free floated off downriver in the raging current. The race was on! Down the shoreline we all sprinted, as fast as we could, hoping to catch up to the loose tow rope.

The first two to drop from exhaustion after four- to five-hundred yards was Gerry and I. A hundred yards later Bret fell to his knees as well. Only my oldest son,

Wayne and Gerry's son, Mark, were still running, frantically, trying to catch up to the floating ATV.

Three-hundred yards later, Wayne collapsed from exhaustion, but then he heard Mark call out from up ahead that he had caught the trailing rope. Mark was a High School long distance track star back in Alberta, Canada and you could sure see why. He just kept going and going like the pink energizer bunny until he got close enough to the tumbling and rolling Argo to leap into the water and grab the rope. However, he couldn't hold it by himself and was being dragged down river with the machine.

Wayne dug deep down within himself and found enough strength to get back up and surge forward to catch up to Mark. They struggled mightily to hold the machine in place, against the surging rapids. Minutes later Bret caught up to them. He was quickly followed by Gerry and me. We were finally able to drag the machine to the gravel-covered shoreline.

So there we were, soaked to the skin and sprawled out like spent salmon lying on the beach. What a run! What a race! When Gerry started laughing, everyone chimed in. It felt good. No one had so much as even smiled for three days before that moment.

We had caught our machine, but what a mechanical mess it was. Once the water had gotten shallow the current had sent the machine tumbling and rolling along the gravel river bottom for several hundred yards before the boys had caught up to it. Fortunately, by this time in life, I had enough experience in the wilds of Alaska to know enough to be prepared for anything and everything. I had plenty of tools and spare parts in the storage compartment for any emergency.

The first thing I did was remove the two spark plugs and watch water shoot out of both cylinders when I cranked the engine over. "Oookay, we tear it down" was my only comment.

I tore the engine and mechanical parts completely apart and cleaned and dried them the best I could. I replaced the points and condenser and after a couple hours work, was able to fire up the engine to everyone's cheers and delight. We had our wheels back again! One of the drive gears was broken, but at least the machine was drivable.

In later years, I actually invented and began manufacturing an all aluminum version of an Argo, which I named the Badger Bush Master. This machine is bigger, tougher and is fully hydrostatic so there are no gears to break.

The last five miles back to our vehicles was uneventful. The storm was over, the sun was out and we had survived our four days of challenges. The two stream crossings went well and by late afternoon, we had our vehicles loaded and were ready to finally head back home.

The storms had washed out huge gullies in the dirt road, but the one-ton, four-wheel-drive truck, equipped with a winch was able to claw its way through.

One last night of camping out, eating the last of our pilot bread and spreadables and we were on our way again bright and early, reaching dry pavement and heading back to Anchorage.

It was August 19. We had been gone twelve days. Three were used to drive there and hike/ferry in to our campsite. We enjoyed one day of hunting, followed by three days of waiting out the storm and five more days to get off the mountain and back home.

We had utilized every bit of survival equipment and back up supplies that we had taken with us. Even our food supply had been exhausted. In fact, everyone that was on that trip has sworn off pilot bread and spreadables for life because that is what we lived on for three whole days.

On our way home, we drove past Robert Service High School in Anchorage, just as the first day of classes were letting out. Bret was supposed to have been there. Oh well.

This sheep hunt adventure had been a true test of character and faith for the five of us. The plan had been a daring one I grant you, but we were experienced outdoorsmen and never attempted anything that wasn't at least plausible. Dangerous yes, but still plausible.

Then the storm hit and changed everything. A once grand adventure filled with excitement and challenge became a pure and simple case for survival. We were tested mentally as well as physically. We had passed the toughness test, and it was Gerry that led us spiritually. His was the calming voice of real faith in the storm while mine was the driving force of never giving up and we needed both voices to survive.

Having since become a man of strong Christian faith, I look back at those treacherous days and can see and feel the presence of God with us. He pulled us through. He gave us the wisdom and strength to survive. It may have been chance that got us into the predicament we found ourselves in, but it wasn't chance that got us out of it.

Catching up to that free-floating ATV which was trailing that tow rope behind it, was nearly an impossible feat. Four, out of the five of us, failed. Being able to even locate and grab the tow rope, due to the providence of shallower water at that very spot, was divine intervention. The tow rope could easily have been floating in the middle of the stream or more likely have become wound up in the rolling machine.

My young nephew, Mark, being able to hang on until the rest of us could get there, was Godly strength, in the time of great need. And being prepared with just the right tools to fix the ATV was God's foresight and provision. Had *other* things broken on the ATV, this story might have a very different ending.

Our Lord was the 6th Person on this trip. He came off the bench and intervened, providing a couple of key miracles.

Prince William Sound

Winters in Alaska are long, excruciatingly long. They start a month earlier than in the northern parts of the "lower forty-eight" and last a month longer. In Alaska, there is a saying that there are only two seasons, "this winter and last winter."

It isn't so much the length of the winters that wears you down, as it is the darkness of them that makes people so stir crazy. On the North Slope, people don't see the sun for three months. In Anchorage, where I lived, the mid-winter sun would come up in the southeast around ten thirty in the morning, hang low 'till about two-thirty in the afternoon and then disappear to the southwest.

In contrast, the mid-summer sun would barely set. If you happened to be driving at midnight you might need your headlights, but you can turn them off by 2:30 a.m.

In winter, all the hunting seasons are over and there are no migrating salmon in the rivers, so life becomes a huge bore for outdoor adventurers like me. I never did well at downhill skiing and the mountains are too dangerous for taking long winter hikes due to the dangers of avalanches, so there I was—stuck indoors.

Reading became my escape. I remember one winter in which I read almost every novel by James Michener including: "Hawaii," "Alaska," "Chesapeake," etc. The next year I got on a Stephen King kick. I read dozens of his spooky freak books, whatever I could find. Once I tired of King, I re-read J.R. Tolkien's trilogy "The Lord of The Rings" and "The Hobbit." I had first found Tolkien back in Junior High School and have loved his works ever since. Frodo and Bilbo Baggins were definitely some adventuresome hobbits—my kind of hobbit for sure!

In the winter of 1984, while in a raging fit of cabin fever induced boredom, I came up with a new idea for adventure—commercial halibut fishing in Prince William Sound. Wow, this was it! Something new and exciting was on the horizon. However, the questions of who, what, when, where and how, needed answers.

The challenge had taken root, so that winter I bought every book I could find on the subject and spent endless hours hounding the Alaska Fish and Game Department to learn everything I could. To secure a license, every commercial vessel needs to have a name. I named the boat the "Foxy Roxy" after my wife, Mary (Uh huh, there is a story here, but I won't go into it).

By spring, I had the gear purchased and the Foxy Roxy rigged and ready to go. I had even talked my good friend, Bill Mailer into joining me. Poor Bill, he had no idea of what he was getting himself into—again!

Long line fishing for halibut in Prince William Sound is definitely a challenge. Halibut are bottom feeders and we fished in waters that were between five-hundred and one-thousand feet deep. Being that the boat, a twenty-one foot Duckworth, was fairly small, we only had room for gear and equipment to put down 1½ -miles of 3/8-inch-diameter, lead-weighted line on the bottom for each set.

We attached clip-on leader lines that were four-feet long. Each was baited with a hook and chunk of herring. These were spaced every six feet along the line. There was a heavy hook anchor with a buoy line attached at each end of the long line so that we could locate our set after soaking it for six hours or so.

In order to pull the heavy line up from the depths, I mounted a stout metal pole with a pulley on it to the deck of the Foxy Roxy. We used ice-climbing cram-pons to grip the lines while pulling them up. With the weight of all the lines, anchors and 1,320 hooked and baited leaders (most of which had a fish on) the pulls were certainly more than a one-man job, but my two sons, Wayne and Bret, plus Bill and I, made a great team.

We kept Bill's 19-foot Gregor tied alongside to toss the fish into once we had them unhooked and "gilled." Once landed, the fish were quickly dispatched with a stout blow to the head (usually with a baseball bat), thus ending any pain immediately, then the gills were slashed to bleed them out (gilled). The larger fish, approximately forty pounds or more, were shot to dispatch them painlessly and quickly, then gaffed before being hauled on board. Dealing with big fish flopping about in a small boat is not a fun thing for you or the fish.

Each season, opening day was a short twenty-four hours, before being closed for varying periods of time, so we tried to get three sets (putting out the baited lead line on bottom) and pulls (hauling the line into the boat) accomplished in that short span of time.

The port we fished out of was in Whittier, Alaska, which is a mere fifty miles south of Anchorage. Without a doubt, Prince William Sound is one of the most beautiful parts of Alaska, or the world for that matter. Snow capped mountain peaks year round, sky-blue clear water surrounding hundreds of flush green islands, and dozens of unnamed glaciers crowding the shorelines of countless dead-end bays.

It is every mariner's paradise and every fisherman's paradise too, as the ocean teems with halibut and salmon. Humpbacked whales, orcas, seals and sea otters abound in Prince William Sound as well, so every trip out is an adventure to treasure forever.

Culrose Passage is a narrow ten-mile-long water-way that connects two larger expanses of open ocean, Port Nellie Juan and Wells Passage. Located approximately thirty miles east of Whittier, this beautiful body of water became our long line halibut fishing grounds.

The twenty-four hour opening day in May of 1984 proved to be a deadly one for Alaska's fishing fleet. A fierce winter storm erupted that evening and three of the largest ships in the fishing fleet sank in the open seas with all hands on board. It was a tragic reminder of just how unforgiving life in the last great frontier can be.

For us "greenhorn hobby fisherman," the storm created a cold and sleepless night but no danger. Unlike the bigger commercial vessels that felt compelled to run their miles and miles of long line throughout the storm and darkness of night, we were content to wait out the storm in a quiet little cove in Culrose Passage.

It was windy, cold and snow was blowing throughout the night. The worst that happened to us was our moorings breaking loose and our boat being blown to the far side of the small bay where we banged against shoreline rocks. Not a real big deal as there was little damage. It was a simple matter to fire up the engine and motor back to the leeward side of the island where we huddled close to shore gaining maximum protection from the wind.

The larger boats that sank that night, were trapped by the storm too far out to sea and had nowhere to escape the raging waves and wind. Most perished due to icing from sea spray, causing massive overweight, a lack of visibility and no ability to keep their vessels facing into the waves and wind correctly. The wind was so strong and waves so rough and high that once their bows were out of position—the boats began to founder. Taking on water and rolling sideways in the trough of a wave is pure suicide. In that position, boats are extremely vulnerable and the next big wave often capsizes them. It is exactly what could have happened to Bill and me when we were stuck in the Cook Inlet storm a few years earlier.

For the most part, our commercial fishing trips to Prince William Sound were wonderful experiences filled with fun and adventure. One June trip, however, proved to be near tragic.

The twenty-four hour opening that month ran from noon one day 'till noon the next and we had hit the jackpot. It seemed like every hook we pulled up had a halibut on it. Usually about 20 percent of the 1,320 hooks would be empty or have lingcod, Irish lord or a salmon shark on them, but all three sets that trip yielded unusually high rates of success.

We had close to three-thousand pounds of halibut on board by the time we pulled anchor to head back to port. We had off-loaded as much gear and fish onto Bill's little 19-foot Gregor as we possibly could, but the twenty-one foot Duckworth was still stuffed beyond capacity.

When I put full throttle to the 351 Ford powered inboard engine, it barely raised the bow a few inches because we were so heavy. This was going to be one long and arduous journey back to Whittier! The Foxy Roxy was basically a riverboat with the engine driving a jet propulsion unit rather than a propeller. This type of drive unit uses about 40 percent of the available horsepower, but is essential for running shallow rivers. In the oceans of Prince William Sound, this loss of power could become deadly.

My friend Bill's boat was an outboard with a pro-peller on it so he could get up on step (skimming along on top of the water) and make fairly good speed. Bill, with my oldest son, Wayne on board, ran ahead for a while and then waited for my son, Bret and me to catch up.

This worked well for one-third of the trip, until we came to Wells Crossing. This was the largest open body of water that we had to traverse, about eight miles across. Bill raced ahead and when he reached the midway point, he radioed back that the waves were at two feet and seemed to be rising, with the wind com-ing off the Harvard Glacier getting stronger rapidly.

I radioed back and told him, "Go ahead and scoot across and wait for us on the leeward side of Pigot Point. We'll be along in due time."

Pigot point was the first land mass on the far side of this wide section of open water that offered a windbreak. Two and even four-foot seas were normally not a problem for the boat to handle, but we were drastically over-loaded and setting much lower in the water than what was safe.

We were only making about three knots-per-hour and by the time we reached the center of Wells Crossing, the waves were between four and six feet. I was quartering into them on the starboard side of the bow and even so, waves were breaking up and over the top of the boat. I knew we were taking on water, so I turned the bilge pump on full blast.

By the time the waves reached six and eight feet, we were really struggling to make any headway. I had to let the wind push us southward to a large extent just to make any sort of headway to the west. This was not fun! I could tell by the way the boat was acting that we were taking on a lot of water, but I couldn't determine how much. We were settling down lower and lower from the weight of the load of halibut and the water we were taking, but I didn't dare to let up on the throttle for fear of nosing down under the next wave.

Bill radioed his concern as he was helplessly watching it unfold before his very eyes. He was in the calmer waters west of Pigot Point where the wind was broken by that land mass and we were still four miles due east in the middle of the open sea and in the grips of the treacherous wind blowing down from the Harvard Glacier some ten miles to the north. The seas were now too high and his boat too small for him to be of any help to us. I told him to hold tight where he was. We were on our own. "I think we can make it, Bill." I radioed back. "But be ready to head our way fast with life preservers at the ready if things get much worse."

That next thirty minute hell ride was one I will never forget. We had taken on so much seawater that it seemed like we were at a stall and barely moving, but we finally reached the shelter from the wind that the Pigot Point land mass provided. The waves had finally settled to only two and three feet. I pulled the throttle back to idle speed to rest the engine (it had been screaming at four-thousand rpm for forty-five minutes) and I was very relieved that we had "made it" but I was completely unprepared for what happened next.

With the lost inertia from our forward thrust, the seawater that we had taken on, rushed to the front and nearly plunged the bow under water. Wow, that was a close call.

Then it hit me, like a balled fist to the stomach. Had I throttled back in six- or eight-foot seas for any reason, we would most assuredly have plunged ourselves to the depths of the ocean in an instant. The on board seawater would have rushed forward, the bow would have plunged downward, the engine would have flooded and stalled and we would have never even had time to jump. We would have dived at a steep angle, like a submerging submarine.

As it was, we were standing knee deep in water in the boat, with the engine completely soaked and dysfunctional. We were dead in the water, but at least we were not dead. Davey Jones would have to wait another day for Bret and me. We didn't go down to his locker after all!

We bailed water 'till the engine was clear, but the wiring was too wet for it to fire up. So, we converted Bills fishing boat to a "water wrecker" and had him tow us the fifteen miles back to Whittier harbor.

People can only last ten to fifteen minutes in the icy waters of Prince William Sound. Had we gone under, and even if Bret and I were able to escape from the cabin of our downed boat, I don't think Bill and Wayne could have reached us in time to save our lives, especially with their little 19-foot boat in eight-foot seas. That is assuming (a big if) they had actually seen us sink and could then find our position on unmarked rough waters.

There is no doubt that our Savior was looking after both of us that day. This was the second time in only two years that my son, Bret and I had been saved at sea by a miracle from God and we were both fully aware of this fact.

By this time, my own personal walk with the Lord was growing stronger. God's many life saving miracles were beginning to jar loose Satan's grip on my soul. God's divine interventions were opening my eyes to His grace and goodness. The spiritual battle for my soul was turning into a raging war of awareness.

My adventuresome life style was continually putting me into dangerous situations that required intervention from God to keep me alive. When the lives of precious friends and loved ones, were repeatedly saved alongside mine, it became so much more important to me than the sparing of my life.

God's life saving miracles were softening me and bringing me closer to Him! I was not only learning to trust in God, but to depend on Him as well. I had always depended on my own skill, but constantly, I had been put in situations where that was not enough. God was making it plain that I needed Him.

Big Mac Publishers

Hugo

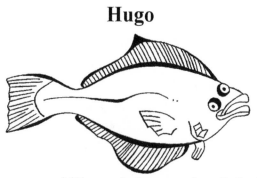

Ever see a killer whale up close? It is quite a thrill. Once when we were docked at an inlet baiting our hooks for the next long line set, the cove suddenly became serenely quiet. The sea otters that had been playing around our boats suddenly and quietly disappeared and even the local sea birds took flight. Then we heard the whissshhh of the three Orcas breathing, as they surfaced not more than fifty yards away from us. There they were, a father, mother and baby Orca, swimming in unison as they cruised down Culrose Passage. My son, Bret quickly grabbed our camera and caught a perfect shot of them surfacing and spraying at the same time. It is an awesome picture!

The most exciting event of our commercial fishing adventures was when we caught Hugo. That is the name I gave to the largest halibut I have ever seen, much less landed. Hugo was a monster, a real denizen of the deep.

When we first caught sight of him, he was just under the boat as we were pulling up the long line. We didn't know if we had a whale or a fish on the hook. He looked bigger than our boat, and he almost was. Our standard procedure was to shoot larger halibut before gaffing them and hoisting on board. The reason for this was twofold. The first was to ensure that the fish was dispatched quickly and as painlessly as possible. The second was for our own safety. Large flopping fish in a small boat can mean disaster, so Hugo presented a problem. Somehow, we needed to get this big monster tired out.

The boat is only six feet wide. One flop from an angry Hugo and we'd be in the water while he'd still be in the boat. *Now what!* We had a dilemma. *What would Captain Ahab do?* I thought. *Better yet, what would Clint Eastwood do?*

"Hang em high," was the answer, so I grabbed a piece of three-eighths inch, nylon anchor rope and crawled over the side of the boat to get at Hugo's head. I slid the rope up from the backside of his gills through his mouth and tied it into a noose like knot. Not fun sticking your hand into the tooth-filled mouth of a five- to six-hundred-pound, angry halibut!

Once secured, we cut the leader line loose and maneuvered Hugo around to the stern of the boat and attached another stout rope to his tail. Then we lifted his tail up out of the water and tied it off on the railing. We "hung em high," so to speak. With his tail in the air, the fish kept trying to swim until he got tired out. When it did tire, we were able to quickly dispatch it with one well-placed shot and hoist it on board without danger to our entire crew. It worked. An hour later, we were finally able to boat our trophy halibut. What a fish! What a great adventure! After that, we finished pulling our set and called it a day. With the addition of Hugo, we already had over a ton of halibut on board.

Miracle in the Wilderness

Big Mac Publishers

Another Miracle In The "Sound"

Salmon fishing in the river and stream systems of Alaska was always a great pleasure and offered countless adventures for my family and me. However, all good things must come to an end they say, and for us it was the advancement of civilization that ruined our fun.

The Susitna River Valley and all our other wilderness places to escape to were getting crowded with people. New boat landings had been built closer to the spawning streams and the city dwellers poured out to them in droves. Jet skis had replaced shallow draft riverboats on the Little Su, which totally ruined any chance of peace and quiet on that once serene body of water. It was time to take our salmon fishing to the ocean, and that meant Prince William Sound.

Twenty years had passed since our last commercial halibut fishing adventure and the Foxy Roxy had long since been sold and renamed, so it was high time to replace her with a new Foxy Roxy II. I decided on a twenty-nine-foot Bayliner Avanti that I found for sale on Lake Winnebago down in Oshkosh, Wisconsin. What a trip that was, towing that 10½-foot-wide, 13,000-pound boat nearly 4,000 miles up the Alcan Highway, and all the way to Whittier, Alaska.

I could write a whole book about that adventure, but suffice it to say, that it was one miserable trip and I would never do it again. I'm still trying to forget about the blown tires, confronting speeding eighteen-wheelers over narrow bridges without guardrails and wide load permit hassles in every Province. Once was enough!

With Evenrude Cobra stern drives, powered by twin .351 CID Ford engines, it soon became apparent to everyone in Whittier, that the Foxy Roxy II was one of the fastest boats on the sound. She would cruise at thirty-five knots, and if you were up for bare foot water skiing, she could top end at nearly fifty mph.

The convertible ragtop she initially had was replaced by a custom-built aluminum cabin after only one summer of fishing adventures. That was because I soon discovered that it is cold and rainy in the Whittier part of Prince William Sound more often than it is sunny and warm.

Surrounded year round by snow capped mountain peaks, Whittier was a deep-water port for submarines during World War II. The near constant cloud and fog cover, caused by the proximity of so many glaciers and mountain peaks in the area, kept the Japanese from discovering our fleet.

After the war ended, the military pulled out and the little town of Whittier emerged. It is now a bustling little tourist trap of a community with over four-hundred, fishing and pleasure boats moored in the harbor.

Several years ago, a dock was built that could handle the largest of ocean liners and that changed the town even more. With the extra commerce that developed from the constant stream of tourists arriving by ship, retail shops sprang up like wildfire and the town actually paved the street(s) and put in dumpsters for trash pick-up. Main Street in Whittier is only one-block long, albeit one very long block.

The salmon runs in this part of Prince William Sound are awesome. There are literally hundreds of fresh water streams that empty into the Sound from the mainland and the dozens of islands found there. Most of these streams play hosts to migrating pink, silver, red and chum salmon for most of the summer months. There is nothing more fun than hooking into salt-water silvers and reds before they find their spawning streams.

The action can be fast and furious, especially if you find a school of big male silvers that typically measure between thirty-two and thirty-five inches in length and weigh between twelve and fifteen pounds. These tail-walking maniacs will definitely get you hooked on fishing "The Sound," that's for sure.

The seas and the weather can change fast in the glacier-riddled coastlines of the Sound. Fortunately, there are plenty of islands and coves to escape from the elements if need be, but a certain amount of navigational aids are necessary for survival.

Number one on the list is a high quality Global Positioning System (GPS) because fog and cloud banks can roll in with little warning. All of the vessels that spend a lot of time in these waters are also equipped with radar units. It is not a necessity, but you definitely do not want to be caught in a shipping lane in zero visibility without one. Shipping lanes are the tracks used by the larger commercial vessels whether they are hauling people or cargo. These are well marked on all nautical charts, but can be hard to locate in bad weather, thus the advantage of having onboard radar.

A book of tide tables is an absolute must as well, but perhaps the best advice I could possibly give to a first time PWS (Prince William Sound) boater is first to slowly and deliberately become familiar with these waters before venturing out too fast and too far.

Get out the cameras and suntan lotion, the sun is shining in Whittier harbor! The day was June 6, 2006 and the temperature was bordering on heat wave status—sixty-five-degrees Fahrenheit.

I had two good friends of mine from Minnesota and their wives with me for a three-day, fishing adventure on the Sound and spirits were as high as that big round yellow thing up in the sky. Even the usually grumpy Harbormaster was in a good mood as we left the port, asking playfully where our water skis were. Foxy Roxy II, with its sleek lines and multi-colored paint scheme definitely looked the part of an over-grown ski boat rather than an Alaskan fishing vessel.

For two full days, the weather held and the fishing was excellent. We limited out on silvers and reds every day with most of the success generated by the women of the group. We even named two parts of Mink Island, Sandy's Bay and Suzy's Point after the two ladies with us. Randy and Joe took a lot of heat over that, but it was in fun.

Day 3 dawned cold, wet and rainy, back to normal conditions for Prince William Sound. After talking with the captain of a small charter boat and getting some valuable information, we decided on a forty-five-mile run to Lone Island to give it a go for halibut that day. After checking the nav' charts, I saw that I was familiar with the first thirty miles of the trip and we had a good GPS to help us find our way for the last fifteen.

Finding halibut in water shallow enough so you could sport fish them was a challenge, but the charter boat captain had done pretty well the day before, so off we went. The waters off the north shore of Lone Island were 200- to 300-feet deep, perfect for bottom fishing with light rod and reel tackle. In water deeper than that, it was too difficult to keep baits near the bottom due to tidal movement and underwater currents.

It was a damp, foggy, rainy overcast day as we traversed through the narrows of Culrose Passage and headed out into the open waters of Port Nellie Juan. We were navigating mostly via GPS at that point, as visibility was less than a quarter mile. Our biggest problem was trying to keep the windshield clear of moisture so we could at least see a little of where we were headed.

Once we entered Port Nellie Juan, the GPS indicated that Perry Island was approximately ten miles to the northeast and Lone Island another five miles east of that. The wind, which was blowing about twenty knots, was out of the northeast and creating seas of four to five feet (waves). Visibility had increased to one-half mile, so we were good if we could keep the windshield clear enough to see past our bow. I had both windshield fans blowing full strength and Randy perched himself up on the dashboard with towels in hand to continually wipe off the fast forming fog and moisture. I decided to dial the GPS out for a wider view so that I could get a better handle on our course. This turned out to be a near fatal decision.

With the GPS dialed out so far, the rocks and boulders that littered the sea floor, as far as five miles south of Perry Island, did not show up on the screen. I was blissfully motoring along without a care in the world, and completely ambivalent to the dangers that lay ahead and below.

Because the seas were a bit choppy, four to five feet, I decided on a course that would take us three or four miles south, which was on the leeward side of Perry Island. The Foxy Roxy II had no problem handling these size rollers, but the passengers were being jostled around a bit. The closer we got to Perry, the calmer the seas became so I put more throttle to the twin .351 Fords and put us up on step at a cruising speed of about thirty-five mph.

Without a doubt, this helped save our lives. With Randy continually trying to wipe the fog off the windshield with a towel, we both strained to see where we were going through the mist and rain, but could never make out more than the ghost-like image of Lone Island looming out of the cloud cover some eight miles ahead.

Then Randy spotted what appeared to be a floating tangle of seaweed or tree branches straight ahead of us. Randy asked, "What is that, a fallen tree or something floating in the water?"

"Where? I can't see a blasted thing."

"Straight ahead! Here let me wipe the windshield for you."

As soon as he did, I saw the rock pile and couldn't believe my eyes. We were at least three miles off the Coast of Perry Island and in the middle of the ocean. How could there be rocks? Nevertheless, there they were, about a ten square foot area of jagged rocks projecting about two-feet high out of the water.

Panic struck in a flash as my heart leapt to my throat. We were less than three of four seconds away from crashing into those jagged rocks! I was going thirty-five mph. There was no way that I could possibly stop in time to avoid them!

Instinctively, I nailed the throttles wide open for *more* speed and turned the controls hard left as far as they would go. This put us into a broadside skid heading into the rocks sideways on the starboard side rather than straight on as we had been before. At this point, I couldn't see the rocks because the boat was tilted sideways in the skid and the rocks were now on my side of the boat, and almost right below me.

When I felt that we were just about to make contact with the outcropping of rocks I swerved hard right which brought the stern about to the left and the bow around to the right and we powered around past the rocks in a half circle free and clear without so much as a scratch on the hull. I remember looking out the side window as we passed the rock formation and headed south at full speed. It was a surreal feeling knowing that certain death for the five of us on board had been miraculously defied.

I dialed the GPS down for a closer look at the waters we were in and was terrified to see that we had just motored through a maze of rocks that littered the shallow sea floor for miles without even knowing it. Randy and I looked at the GPS and then at each other in total silence. No words needed to be spoken.

Our other three passengers were still in the rear seat joking and laughing; they were completely unaware of the narrow escape we had just had, so we decided to leave it that way. To this day, I wonder how close we really did come to hitting those rocks. Was it inches, or less than an inch? Or, how about those submerged rocks that never broke the water's surface, but were there just the same? It was undoubtedly God's meticulous planning that the tide was at its highest point at the time. How close had I come to the many other rocks I blithely steered the boat over, not even knowing they were there? God was truly my co-captain.

Randy and I both know that God saved our lives. There was no luck involved. He was the one that told me to *accelerate of all things*, and *when* to make the turns to avoid those rocks and He was the one that directed our path out to safety. It was definitely a miracle that we didn't crash, and at thirty-five mph the boat would have shattered into a million pieces. There would have been no chance of surviving the icy waters of the North Pacific. This miracle, more than any other, became life changing for me.

Miracle in the Wilderness

200
Big Mac Publishers

God Is Love

I was sixty-two years old when God saved my life with that miracle near Perry Island. That near death experience really caused me to pause and ponder about the direction of my life. As of this writing, God has saved me from certain death no less than nine times with His miracles in the wilderness, plus a whole bunch more times when he lent a much-needed helping hand to get me out of other jams that I had gotten myself into, all in the name of adventure.

Was I taking too much of a risk that day when I ventured into that rock strewn coastline off Perry Island? Four other lives could have been lost that day because of my actions. Yes, it would have been an accident, but it would have been an accident that could have been prevented by me. I was the one driving the boat and I was the one reading the GPS that day, so I was the reason that God had to intervene.

I could be wrong, but it seems to me that God spends much more time getting us out of dire situations than he does putting us into them. I am quite sure that God didn't purposely cause the windstorm that got my friend Bill and I caught in those forty-foot seas in Cook Inlet a few years earlier, but it definitely was His doing that kept Bill's motor running until we reached safety. Not that He couldn't have controlled the seas, after all he quieted them in Mark 4:39 and walked on them in John 6:19.

I also don't think that God purposely had me wonder into that grassy meadow in the wilds of Canada that had three, adult-sized, grizzly bears in it, but I know beyond any doubt that He caused the strong wind to blow from the bears toward me (thus sending my scent away from them and creating extra noise) so that I could escape with my life. Moreover, how about that near crash with my airplane out in Wyoming? Only a few seconds made the difference between life and death there and I had nothing to do with the engine suddenly coming to full life at the right time, but someone did.

Yes, I am convinced that God can do anything. He is, after all, the Creator of the universe. I also believe that God does occasionally create hardships to teach us lessons intended to bring us closer to Him. For the most part though, I think we get ourselves into tough situations on our own and need Him to save our lives.

This brings me back to the question of, "Why me?" Why *was* God continually saving my life? In Cook Inlet was He really saving me or was I simply along for the ride as He intervened to save my three companions? Or, how about that danger packed Dahl sheep hunt in the Wrangle Mountains? Who was really saved there, and why?

The answers to these and many other questions were answered for me on March 30, 1996. That is the day that the Holy Spirit brought me truth. That is the date of my rebirth into the kingdom of God. That was the date of miracle number ten in my life. It was the most important miracle of them all. It was the day the Lord saved me for eternity.

I had been living most of my life as a "Tweener." Tweener is a word that our Christian study group, which meets weekly at our home in Wisconsin, uses for a person who considers himself a Christian, goes to church regularly, conscientiously tries to do what is right, but has not yet given his soul to the Lord. He is "between" believing what he ascertains as true and actually knowing truth. The spirit of the Lord does not dwell in him, yet he believes that he is a member of God's family.

A Tweener is someone that believes in Jesus, but does not follow Him. Jesus says in Matthew 7:21, "Not everyone who says to me 'Lord, Lord' will enter the kingdom of heaven, but only he who does the will of my Father who is in heaven."

Many of us go through our entire lives believing that we are living a Godly life, but in truth, we are only deceiving ourselves. The truth cannot be fully known until one's heart is given over to God *and* He graciously allows the Holy Spirit to enter our souls. We must take the first step to come to Him and then it is His miracle that saves us for eternity.

That is exactly what happened to me on March 30, 1996. Once again, I had been struggling. I was trying to control my life and my surroundings with my wishes and my ideas until I finally gave up and went to the Lord in total submission and prayer. While home alone that day, I threw myself onto the living room floor and cried out to the Lord for help. I begged for forgiveness and pleaded for mercy "I cannot do this alone any more, Lord" I confessed. "God, I *need* you so badly."

Deep inside, I knew that I had completely given myself over to Him 100 per cent and had put all of my trust in Him. I spread my arms heavenward in total submission to His will. He answered me with a voice in my head that was almost deafening, "Life is all about love, Tom and GOD IS LOVE."

That was my message and that was all I needed to hear. 1John 4:8 says, "Whoever does not love does not know God, because God is love." I immediately had the weight of the world lifted off my heart. I was finally at peace. The Holy Spirit was now dwelling in me. II Corinthians 5:17 says, "Therefore, if anyone is in Christ, he is a new creation; the old has gone, the new has come!" I had finally broken the hard outer layer of individualism apart from God and begun a new oneness with Him. From this point on God was in control and I would trust Him with everything in my life.

I learned truth that day. He saved me from the icy waters of the North Pacific because he loves me. He saved my companions because He loves them, too. He saved me from so many certain death situations because He was not finished with me yet. God may give us our second (and maybe more) chances so that we may not only just live, but live for Him! We are alive to serve Him by loving and doing good for others. But, how many chances will you have? Would I have had any more if I had not responded?

The spirit world is real. Satan does exist, and he did not let me go without a struggle. For days and weeks on end, he kept bringing thoughts of doubt into my mind. He just would not leave me alone. Unfortunately, my pastor at the time did not believe my story of transformation. He passed it off as an over-emotional moment caused by undue stress. Satan loves to use doubters to derail us.

My very strong in Christian faith brother, Gerry was not influenced by Satan, however. He was over-joyed with my newfound faith and was a big help to me during the temptations that came my way.

I needed a mentor, but Gerry lived two-thousand miles away in Edmonton, Alberta, Canada, so I learned to call on Jesus directly when I needed help. Every time that I would feel the presence of the evil one trying to negatively influence my faith, all I had to do was call on the Lord for deliverance, and He never failed me. I couldn't do it alone; I always had to call out His name in order to chase the evil spirit from me.

Then, in the middle of one memorable night, I experienced the most astonishing event of my life. I suddenly awoke, abruptly sat up in bed and shouted loudly in a voice that wasn't mine, *"Get thee gone Satan and never to return!"* I was covered with sweat and had the strong taste of bile in my mouth.

My wife was startled and scared because she knew that deep sounding voice with the ancient dialect she heard was not mine. I began shaking from exhaustion and wept tears of joy because I knew that the battle for my soul was over. I could feel it. I believe it was an Angel of the Lord that had spoken out through me. Who else could it have been?

Satan was defeated, that much was certain. I now fully and completely belonged to God. The feeling I had was like the words of that popular song, "Amazing Grace (My Chains Are Gone)": "My chains are gone / I've been set free / My God, my Savior has ransomed me / And like a flood His mercy reigns / Unending love Amazing Grace / I am forever His!"

The evil one still does take runs at my soul yet to this day, but he never gets very far. Don't get me wrong, I am not sin free, far from it. The temptations still come, but I am able to recognize Satan's efforts at deception much easier now and know that I can call on the Lord at any time to rid myself of his influence. By the grace of God, I am a saved Christian. This is the most wonderful feeling a person can have.

A short time after I became reborn into the faith, my mom's husband, Al became seriously ill. He had been battling congestive heart failure on and off for several years, but this time the end was imminent. Mom and Al had married while I was in college. As a matter of fact, I first met my wife, Mary at their wedding back in 1965. Al was truly a wonderful God-fearing man. He was kind, gentle and always wore a smile on his face.

He gave Mom all the love and happiness that she so richly deserved. They had a wonderful marriage, but knowing that he was nearing death, Al was very troubled over what was to become of Mom after he was gone. Mom had been struggling with Alzheimer's disease for several years and Al was her sole caregiver. He loved her dearly and his heart ached over fear of what would become of her after he left this earth.

I was the only one of her three sons that lived in the area and as far as Al knew, I was not a saved Christian. He had little confidence in me and was heartbroken that he would not be able to continue on caring for Mom. I went to his bedside at the hospital one night and could feel his despair.

I held him tightly and told him of my newfound faith in God. I remember him looking deeply into my eyes and could feel it in my heart that he knew that the Holy Spirit did dwell in me. I promised Al that I would never let Mom down and would always be there for her. I could tell that Al trusted me once he knew that I trusted in the Lord. It was a good feeling. Al Opsal died in peace early that morning, June 1, 1996.

Mom lived for another six years, battling Alzheimer's disease every step of the way. My wife, Mary loved Mom and Al deeply, too, and was most instrumental in helping care for Mom those last tough years. Mary still carries Mom's old cane around in the trunk of her car as a reminder of the many wonderful days they had spent together. I was holding her hand when she breathed her last and went to be with our Lord on May 5, 2002. What a tremendous honor that was.

So, why did God save me with so many miracles throughout my life? There are two parts to the answer. First, He loves me just as He loves all of us. According to scripture, it is a love so great that it passes all understanding.

Second, He saved me so that I could be of service to Him. He needed me to be there for Mom and Al, two of His loyal and loving servants in their times of need. He saved me so that I can continue to be here for my family and everyone else that my life touches.

We are *ALL* here to do good things for others to the glory of God our Father. It is what we do as born-again Christians. It is our way of life. It is our calling. This is God's purpose in life for us. **GOD IS LOVE!** Once we are His, we can serve Him. I invite you to come to Him, accept His love and serve Him with me

About the Author

Tom Lynch: Author, Adventurer, Pilot, Christian, Husband, Father, Grandfather, Businessman, Hunter, Fisherman and Sourdough.

Tom Lynch and Mary Jo, his wife of forty-four years, live on Lake Wisconsin near the town of Lodi.

"Once you have lived in Alaska you can never leave it forever," believes Tom.

Big Mac Publishers

The beauty, majesty, wildness of the land and the independent spirit of the people make Alaska, our countries "last great frontier," very special.

If you are a lover of the outdoors and enjoy adventure of all kinds, Alaska is the place for you. Tom returns every year to hunt, to fish and simply be a part of *alayeksa* the great country.

Special Acknowledgements

Gerry, my brother in faith as well as real life has always been an inspiration to me. Thank you Ger for teaching me how to hunt and survive in the wilderness. *See anything lately?*

Craig Heilman, a very dear pastor and mission's field friend of mine gave me wonderful advice, assistance and encouragement to continue on and finish this book.

My two oldest sons, Wayne and Bret, who managed to live through many wild adventures with me, were a tremendous encouragement. So were Mary Jo, Kelly Jo and Adam Joseph, even though they were never involved in any life threatening situations with me. Unless you count that one wild ride down the Susitna River rapids with a busted motor or that time when I almost rolled our motor home over in the ditch near Wild Horse, Montana as life threatening . . . Hmm, maybe another book is in order.

A special thank you to Greg Bilbo McElveen my publisher/editor. Without your help, patience and faith *Miracles* would never have become reality. How God put us together certainly shows how He works in mysterious ways, doesn't it.

Most of all thanks to my Lord and Savior Jesus Christ for rescuing me, standing by me and being so patient with me. Thank you for blessing me with Mary Jo, my beautiful wife of forty-four years. You are an *Awesome* God!